Sarah Morgan Bryan Piatt

**Poems**

Sarah Morgan Bryan Piatt

**Poems**

ISBN/EAN: 9783744714549

Printed in Europe, USA, Canada, Australia, Japan

Cover: Foto ©Thomas Meinert / pixelio.de

More available books at **www.hansebooks.com**

# POEMS

BY

## SARAH PIATT

VOL. I

LONDON
LONGMANS, GREEN AND CO.
AND NEW YORK: 15 EAST 16TH STREET
1894

*[All rights reserved]*

These two volumes comprise all of the Author's poems hitherto published in this country, with the exception of those referring to her residence in Ireland entitled "An Enchanted Castle and Other Poems." Many additional pieces, however, are also included.

J. J. P.

TO

## MY NEAREST NEIGHBOUR.

Loved as myself—and more!
This book is yours, not mine, to give or take.
Your hand, not mine, has sent it from your door.
My heart goes with it—only for your sake.

# CONTENTS

|  | PAGE |
|---|---|
| DEDICATION, | iii |

NARRATIVE PIECES :—

| A Voyage to the Fortunate Isles, | 3 |
|---|---|
| "Folded Hands," | 10 |
| The Longest Death-Watch, | 12 |
| Two Veils, | 17 |
| Tradition of Conquest, | 19 |
| The Black Princess, | 21 |
| Aunt Annie, | 24 |
| Life or Love, | 27 |
| Two Blush-Roses, | 29 |
| The Gift of Empty Hands, | 31 |
| The King's Memento Mori, | 33 |
| The Brother's Hand, | 34 |
| The Last Angel, | 51 |

DRAMATIC PERSONS AND MOODS :—

| The Fancy Ball, | 55 |
|---|---|
| Twelve Hours Apart, | 56 |
| A Lily of the Nile, | 58 |
| There was a Rose, | 60 |
| If I were a Queen, | 62 |

A

## CONTENTS.

|  | PAGE |
|---|---|
| Sometime, | 68 |
| The Order for her Portrait, | 70 |
| The Clothes of a Ghost, | 71 |
| Flight, | 73 |
| Marble or Dust? | 75 |
| Their Lost Picture, | 77 |
| The Palace-Burner, | 78 |
| A Masked Ball, | 80 |
| A Doubt, | 82 |
| A Woman's Birthday, | 84 |
| Comfort—By a Coffin, | 86 |
| We Two, | 88 |
| Enchanted, | 89 |
| The Altar at Athens, | 91 |
| Her Cross and Mine, | 92 |
| Two in Two Worlds, | 94 |
| Caprice at Home, | 96 |
| A Wall Between, | 98 |
| A Lesson in a Picture, | 108 |
| From Two Windows, | 110 |
| Denied, | 111 |
| After the Quarrel, | 113 |
| The Descent of the Angel, | 115 |
| Double Quatrains, | 116 |

IN COMPANY WITH CHILDREN:—

|  |  |
|---|---|
| After Wings, | 125 |
| Baby or Bird? | 126 |
| My Babes in the Wood, | 127 |
| My Ghost, | 129 |

CONTENTS. vii

| | PAGE |
|---|---|
| The End of the Rainbow, | 131 |
| The Highest Mountain, | 132 |
| Playing Beggars, | 133 |
| A Child's First Sight of Snow, | 136 |
| Last Words, | 136 |
| My Artist, | 138 |
| The Sad Story of a Little Girl, | 141 |
| At Hans Andersen's Funeral, | 143 |
| A Coat-of-Arms, | 146 |
| Hiding the Baby, | 150 |
| The Little Boy I Dreamed about, | 153 |
| Calling the Dead, | 156 |
| The Lamb in the Sky, | 157 |
| "I Want it Yesterday," | 158 |
| Into the World and Out, | 158 |
| The Baby's Brother, | 159 |
| Child's-Faith, | 160 |
| The Funeral of a Doll, | 161 |
| One Year Old, | 163 |
| About a Magician, | 164 |
| Forgiveness, | 165 |
| Everything, | 166 |
| Little Christian's Trouble, | 167 |
| Midsummer-Night Fairies, | 168 |

MISCELLANEOUS:—

| | |
|---|---|
| Hearing the Battle, | 171 |
| To-day, | 172 |
| Shapes of a Soul, | 174 |
| Stone for a Statue, | 175 |

## CONTENTS.

| | PAGE |
|---|---|
| "I wish that I could go," | 176 |
| Counting the Graves, | 179 |
| A Dead Man's Friends, | 181 |
| His Share and Mine, | 182 |
| The Bird in the Brain, | 184 |
| A Prettier Book, | 186 |
| Asking for Tears, | 188 |
| "A Letter from To-morrow," | 189 |
| The Dead Book, | 192 |

Songs :—

| | |
|---|---|
| Reproof to a Rose, | 195 |
| When the Full Moon's Light is Burning, | 196 |
| The Song no Bird should Sing in Vain, | 197 |
| Come, Wailing Winds; come, Birds of Night | 198 |
| Sad Spring-Song, | 199 |
| Say the Sweet Words, | 200 |
| Fulfilment, | 201 |
| Good-bye, | 202 |
| Life and Death, | 203 |
| Making Peace, | 204 |

# NARRATIVE PIECES.

# A VOYAGE TO THE FORTUNATE ISLES.

### THE FABLE OF A HOUSEHOLD.

"YES, but I fear to leave the shore.
  So fierce, so shadowy, so cold,
Deserts of water lie before—
  Whose secrets night has never told,
Save in close whispers to the dead.
  I fear," one vaguely said.

One answered: " Will you waver here?
  As wild and lonesome as the things
Which hold their wet nests, year by year,
  In these poor rocks, are we. Their wings
Grow restless—wherefore not our feet?
  That which is strange is sweet."

"That which we know is sweeter yet.
  Do we not love the near Earth more

Than the far Heaven ? Does not Regret
Walk with us, always, from the door
That shuts behind us, though we leave
    Not much to make us grieve ? "


" Why fret me longer, when you know
    Our hands with thorny toil are torn ?
Scant bread and bitter, heat and snow,
    Rude garments, souls too blind and worn
To climb to Christ for comfort : these
    Are here. And there—the Seas.


" True, our great Lord will let us drink
    At some wild springs, and even take
A few slight dew-flowers. But, I think,
    He cares not how our hearts may ache.
He comes not to the peasant's hut
    To learn—the door is shut.


" Oh, He is an hard Master. Still
    In His rough fields, for piteous hire,
To break dry clods is not my will.
    I thank Him that my arms can tire.
Let thistles henceforth grow like grain,
    To mock His sun and rain.

"Others He lifts to high estate—
    Others, no peers of yours or mine.
He folds them in a silken fate,
    Casts pearls before them—oh, the swine!
Drugs them with wine, veils them with lace;
    And gives us this mean place."


"Well. May there not be butterflies
    That lift with weary wings the air;
That loathe the foreign sun, which lies
    On all their colours like despair;
That glitter, home-sick for the form
    And lost sleep of the worm?"


"Hush—see the ship. It comes at last,"
    She whispered, through forlornest smiles:
"How brave it is! It sails so fast.
    It takes us to the Fortunate Isles.
Come." Then the heart's great silence drew
    Like Death around the Two.


Death-like it was—through pain and doubt,
    To leave their world at once and go,
Pale, mute, and even unconscious, out
    Through dimness toward some distant Glow,

That might be but Illusion caught
  In the fine net of Thought.

As ghosts, led by a ghostly sleep—
  Followed by Life, a breathless dream—
Out in eternal dusk, that keep
  Their way somewhere, these Two did seem,
Till the sea-moon climbed to her place
  And looked in each still face.

"The worm," she waking said, "must long
  To put on beauty and to fly,
But"——coming toward them sad and strong,
  There was a little double cry.
"What hurts the children ? They should rest,
  In such a floating nest."

"Oh, Mother, look—we all are gone.
  Our house is swimming in the sea.
It will not stop. It keeps right on.
  How far away we all must be !
The wind has blown it from the cliff.
  It rocks us like a skiff.

"We all will drown but Baby. He
  Is in his pretty grave so far.

He has to sleep till Judgment. We
  Must sink where all the sailors are,
Who used to die, when storms would come,
  Away off from their home."

"Lie still, you foolish yellow heads.
  This is a ship. We're sailing." "Where?"
"Go nestle in your little beds.
  Be quiet. We shall soon be there."
"Where?" "Why, it is not many miles."
  "Where?" "To the Fortunate Isles."

"Home is the best. Oh, what a light!
  God must be looking in the sea.
It is His glass. He makes it bright
  All over with His face. And He
Is angry. He is talking loud
  Out of that broken cloud.

"The men all hear Him, in the ropes:
  He's telling them the ship must go.
They'd better climb to Him." Pale Hopes
    Looked from each wretched breast, to know
If somewhere, through the shattered night,
  One sail could be in sight.

And Two, who waited, dying slow,
    Said, clinging to their desperate calm :
"We had not thought such wind could blow
    Out of the warm leaves of the palm.
Strange, with the Fortunate Isles so nigh—
    Strange, cruel, thus to die."


"The Fortunate Isles?" one other cried;
    "You knew we were not sailing there?
They lie far back across the tide.
    Their cliffs are grey and wet and bare;
And quiet people in their soil
    Are still content to toil.


"Toward shining snakes, toward fair dumb birds,
    Toward Fever hiding in the spice,
We voyaged." But his tropic words
    Dropped icy upon hearts of ice.
The lonesome gulf to which they passed
    Had shown the Truth at last.


That wavering glare the drowning see,
    With phantoms of their life therein,
Flashed on them both. Yet mostly she
    Felt all her sorrow, all her sin,

And learned, most bitterly, how dear
    Their crags and valleys were.


Their home, whose dim wet windows stared
    Through drops of brine, like eyes through tears;
The blue ground-blossoms that had cared
    To creep about their feet for years;
And their one grave so deep, so small—
    Sinking, they saw them all!


To leave the Fortunate Isles, away
    On the other side of the world, and sail
Still further from them, day by day,
    Dreaming to find them; and to fail
In knowing, till the very last,
    They held one's own sweet Past:


Such lot was theirs. Such lot will be,
    Ah, much I fear me, yours and mine.
Because our air is cold, and we
    See Summer in some mirage shine,
We leave the Fortunate Isles behind,
    The Fortunate Isles to find.

# "FOLDED HANDS."

#### THE STORY OF A PICTURE.

MADONNA eyes looked at him from the air,
   But never from the picture.  Still he painted.
The hovering halo would not touch the hair ;
   The patient saint still stared at him—unsainted.

Day after day flashed by in flower and frost ;
   Night after night, how fast the stars kept burning
His little light away, till all was lost !—
   All, save the bitter sweetness of his yearning.

Slowly he saw his work : it was not good.
   Ah, hopeless hope !  Ah, fiercely-dying passion !
"I am no painter," moaned he as he stood,
   With folded hands in death's unconscious fashion.

"Stand as you are, an instant !" some one cried.
   He felt the voice of a diviner brother.
The man who was a painter, at his side,
   Showed how his folded hands could serve another.

Ah, strange, sad world, where Albert Dürer takes
The hands that Albert Dürer's friend has folded,
And with their helpless help such triumph makes!—
Strange, since both men of kindred dust were moulded.

# THE LONGEST DEATH-WATCH.[1]

THE woman is a picture now.
   The Spanish suns have touched her face;
   The coil of gold upon her brow
     Shines back on an Imperial race
     With most forlorn and bitter grace.

Old palace-lamps behind her burn,
   The ermine moulders on her train.
Her ever-constant eyes still yearn
     For one who came not back to Spain;
     And dim and hollow is her brain.

One only thing she knew in life,
   Four hundred ghostly years ago—
That she was Flemish Philip's wife.
     Nor much beyond she cared to know;
     Without a voice she tells me so.

[1] Joanna, the wife of Philip the Handsome, was the daughter of Ferdinand and Isabella, sister of Catherine of Aragon, and mother of the Emperor Charles V.

Philip the Beautiful—whose eyes
   Might win a woman's heart, I fear,
Even from his grave! "He will arise,"
   The monks had murmured by his bier,
   "And reign once more among us here."


She heard their whisper, and forgot
   Castile and Aragon, and all
Save Philip, who had loved her not;
   The cruel darkness of his pall
   Seemed on an empty world to fall.


She took the dead man—to her sight
   A prince in death's disguise, as fair
As when his wayward smile could light
   The throne he wedded her to share—
   And followed, hardly knowing where.


Almost as dumb as he, she fled,
   Pallid and wasted, toward the place
Where he, the priestly promise said,
   Must wait the hour when God's sweet grace
   Should breathe into his breathless face.

Once, when the night was weird with rain,
   She sought a convent's shelter. When
The tapers showed a veiléd train
   Of nuns, instead of cowléd men,
   She stole into the night again:


"These women, sainted though they be,"
   She moaned through all her jealous mind,
"Are women still, and shall not see
   Philip the Fair—though he is blind!
   Favour with him I yet shall find."


Then, with her piteous yearning wild:
   "Unclose his coffin quick, I pray."
Fiercely the sudden lightning smiled—
   When they had laid the lid away—
   Like scorn, upon the regal clay.


She kissed the dead of many days,
   As though he were an hour asleep.
Dark men with swords to guard her way
   Wept for her—but she did not weep;
   She had her vigil still to keep.

They reached the appointed cloister. While
    The heart of Philip withering lay,
She, without moan, or tear, or smile,
    Watched from her window, legends say—
    Watched seven-and-forty years away!


Winds blew the blossoms to and fro,
    Into the world and out again :
" He will come back to me, I know "—
    Poor whisper of a wandering brain
    To peerless patience, peerless pain !


. . . Ah, longest, loneliest, saddest tryst
    Was ever kept on earth ! And yet
Had he arisen would he have kissed
    The grey wan woman he had met,
    Or—taught her how the dead forget ?


Could she have won, discrowned and old,
    The love she could not win, in sooth,
When queenly purple, fold on fold,
    And all the subtle grace of youth,
    Helped her to hide a hapless truth ?

Did she not fancy—should she see
That coffin, watched so long, unclose—
The royal tenant there would be
    Still young, still fair, when he arose,
    Beside her withered leaves and snows?


He would have laughed to breathe the tale
    Of this crazed stranger's love, I fear,
To moon and rose and nightingale,
    With courtly jewels glimmering near,
    Into some lovely lady's ear.

## TWO VEILS.

From the nun's wan life a buried passion
   Blossomed like a grave-rose in her face;
"Sweet, my child," she said, "in what fair fashion
   Do you mean to wear this lovely lace?

"Thus?"—and, with a feverish hand and shaken,
   Round her head the precious veil she wound.
"Faith in man," she said, "I have forsaken;
   Faith in God most surely I have found.

"Yet with music in the dewy distance,
   And the whole world flowering at my feet,
Through this convent-garment's dark resistance
   Backward I can hear my fierce heart beat.

"Tropic eyes too full of light and languor,
   Northern soul too grey with Northern frost:
Ashes—ashes after fires of anger!
   Love and beauty—what a world I lost!"

"Sister," laughed the girl with girlish laughter,
  "Sister, do you envy me my veil?"
'You may come to ask for mine hereafter,"
  Answered very piteous lips and pale.

" No, for your black cross is heavy bearing;
  Tiresome counting these stone beads must be.
Oh, but there are jewels worth the wearing
  Waiting in the sunny world for me!

. . . "Sister, have a care—you are forgetting.
  Do not broider thorns among my flowers—
Only buds and leaves: your tears are wetting
  All my bridal lace." They fell in showers.

After years and years, beside the grating,
  (Oh, that saddest sight, young hair grown grey!)
With dry boughs and empty winds awaiting
  At the cloister door, came one to pray.

"Sister, see my bride-veil! there was never
  Thorn so sharp as those within its lace.
Sister, give me yours to wear for ever;
  Give me yours, and let me hide my face."

## TRADITION OF CONQUEST.

His Grace of Marlborough, legends say,
   Though battle-lightnings proved his worth,
Was scathed like others, in his day,
   By fiercer fires at his own hearth.

The patient chief, thus sadly tried—
   Madam, the Duchess, was so fair—
In Blenheim's honours felt less pride
   Than in the lady's lovely hair.

Once, (shorn, she had coiled it there to wound
   Her lord when he should pass, 'tis said,)
Shining across his path he found
   The glory of the woman's head.

No sudden word, nor sullen look,
   In all his after days, confessed
He missed the charm whose absence took
   A scar's pale shape within his breast.

I think she longed to have him blame,
    And soothe him with imperious tears :—
As if her beauty were the same,
    He praised her through his courteous years.


But, when the soldier's arm was dust,
    Among the dead man's treasures, where
He laid it as from moth and rust,
    They found his wayward wife's sweet hair.

# THE BLACK PRINCESS.

### A TRUE FABLE OF MY OLD KENTUCKY NURSE.

I KNEW a Princess : she was old,
   Crisp-haired, flat-featured, with a look
Such as no dainty pen of gold
   Would write of in a Fairy Book.

So bent she almost crouched, her face
   Was like the Sphinx's face, to me,
Touched with vast patience, desert grace,
   And lonesome, brooding mystery.

What wonder that a faith so strong
   As hers, so sorrowful, so still,
Should watch in bitter sands so long,
   Obedient to a burdening will!

This Princess was a Slave—like one
   I read of in a painted tale;
Yet free enough to see the sun,
   And all the flowers, without a veil.

Not of the Lamp, not of the Ring,
    The helpless, powerful Slave was she,
But of a subtler, fiercer Thing:
    She was the Slave of Slavery.


Court-lace nor jewels had she seen:
    She wore a precious smile, so rare
That at her side the whitest queen
    Were dark—her darkness was so fair.


Nothing of loveliest loveliness
    This strange, sad Princess seemed to lack;
Majestic with her calm distress
    She was, and beautiful though black:


Black, but enchanted black, and shut
    In some vague Giant's tower of air,
Built higher than her hope was. But
    The True Knight came and found her there.


The Knight of the Pale Horse, he laid
    His shadowy lance against the spell
That hid her Self: as if afraid,
    The cruel blackness shrank and fell.

Then, lifting slow her pleasant sleep,
  He took her with him through the night,
And swam a River cold and deep,
  And vanished up an awful Height.

And, in her Father's House beyond,
  They gave her beauty robe and crown :
——On me, I think, far, faint, and fond,
  Her eyes to-day look, yearning, down.

## AUNT ANNIE.

THE old house has, for being sweet,
    Some sweeter reason than the rose
Which, red or white, about the feet
    Of many a nested home-bird grows.


And sadder reason than the rain
    On the quaint porch, for being sad,
(Oh, human pity, human pain!)
    The old house, in its shadows, had.


I sat within it as a guest,
    I who went from it as a wife;—
The young days there, though not the best,
    Had been the fairest of my life:


For love itself must ever seem
    More precious, to our restless youth,
When hovering subtly in its dream
    Than when we touch its nestling truth.

## AUNT ANNIE.

I sat there as a guest, I said—
   Holding the loveliest boy on earth,
With his fair, sleepy, yellow head
   Close to the pleasant shining hearth.


He laughed out in his sleep, and I
   Laughed too, and kissed him—when I heard
A wise and very cautious sigh;
   And once again the dimples stirred.


Aunt Annie looked at him awhile;
   Then shook her head at her own fears,
With more of sorrow in her smile
   Than I could ever put in tears.


"He *is* a pretty boy I know—
   The prettiest in the world? Ah, me!
One other, fifty years ago,
   Was quite as pretty, dear, as he.


"Now I am eighty. Twenty-five
   Are gone since last we heard from James.
I sometimes think he is alive."
   She hushed, and looked into the flames.

"He used to tell me, when a child,
    Of far, strange countries, where they say
The flowers bloom all the year"—she smiled—
    "I can't believe it, to this day!

"And still I think he may have crossed
    The sea—and stayed the other side.
His letters may have all been lost—
    Who knows? Who knows? The world is wide.

"I often think, if you could know
    How much he makes me think of *him*,
You 'd guess why I love Victor so."
    Again the troubled eyes were dim.

"If your child, such a night, were out
    Lost in this dark and snow and sleet,
You would go wild, I do not doubt."
    I almost heard her own heart beat.

"Yet long, on stormier nights than this,
    Mine has been out—why should I care
How many a winter now it is?
    Mine has been out—and He knows where."

## LIFE OR LOVE.

"OH, world so beautiful, could we hide
   Somewhere in your flowers from death!"
A wandering voice in a palace sighed,
   Where the East-rose draws her breath.

"Ah, jewels have passed through yon fires of mine,
   Worth Persia ten times told;
And the essence that makes our dust divine
   Is here in this cup of gold:"

And the Master knelt with a beard that rushed
   To his feet like a storm of snow.
But Youth in his bosom yearned and flushed,
   And Youth in his voice spake low.

Yet the queen lay dark on the gorgeous floor,
   With her eyes hid in her hair.
"Should she lift her face from the dust any more,"
   They moaned, "it will not be fair:

"All night, with the moon, she watches and weeps;
   No song in her ear is sweet.

All day, like the dead king's shadow, she keeps
　　Her place at the dead king's feet."

"Your beauty is worth all other things.
　　The insolent gods have seen.
It should not fade—for a thousand kings.
　　You shall be for ever the queen."

And closer the Master held the charm:
　　"It is Life, O queen, that I bring."
She reached the cup with a wandering arm:
　　"Is it Life—for my lord, the king?"

"Nay, the king will not drink wine to-day.
　　There is one drop here—for you.
Oh, listen, and keep your beauty, I pray,
　　While the sweet world keeps the dew.

"For you, new lovers shall always rise;"
　　And the lords and the princes near,
With the sunrise-light in their Persian eyes,
　　Stood, jewelled and still, to hear.

"Oh, what were Life to the lonely—what?
　　It is Love I would have you bring,
And Love in this widowed world is not.
　　Let me go to my lord, the king."

## TWO BLUSH-ROSES.

A BLUSH-ROSE lay in the summer;
   There were golden lights in the sky,
And a woman saw the blossom,
   As she stood with her lover nigh.

A band in the flowering distance
   Played a dreamy Italian air,
Like a memory changed to music,
   And it drifted everywhere.

'Twas an exiled love of its Southland,
   That air, and its delicate wails
Were only the wandering echoes
   Of the songs of nightingales.

"I love you," he tenderly whispered;
   "I love you," she answered as low:
And the music grew sweeter and sweeter,
   Because it had listened, I know.

But she looked at the rose in the summer,
  And said, with a tremulous tear,
"The love that now beats in my bosom
  Will bloom in a blush-rose next year."


A blush-rose lay in the summer;
  There were golden lights in the sky,
And a woman saw the blossom,
  As she stood with her lover nigh.


The band in the flowering distance
  Played the dreamy Italian air,
Like a memory changed to music,
  And it drifted everywhere.


"I love you," he tenderly whispered;
  "I love you," she timidly said:
And the music grew sadder and sadder,
  And the blush-rose before them dropped dead.


Then he knew that the music remembered,
  And knew the love that had beat
Last year in her beautiful bosom
  Lay dead in the rose at his feet.

# THE GIFT OF EMPTY HANDS.

### A FAIRY TALE.

THEY were two princes doomed to death;
Each loved his beauty and his breath:
"Leave us our life, and we will bring
Fair gifts unto our lord, the King."

They went together. In the dew
A charmèd bird before them flew.
Through sun and thorn one followed it;
Upon the other's arm it lit.

A rose, whose faintest flush was worth
All buds that ever blew on earth,
One climbed the rocks to reach; ah! well,
Into the other's breast it fell.

Weird jewels, such as fairies wear,
When moons go out, to light their hair,
One tried to touch on ghostly ground;
Gems of quick fire the other found.

One with the dragon fought, to gain
The enchanted fruit, and fought in vain;
The other breathed the garden's air,
And gathered precious apples there.

Backward to the imperial gate
One took his fortune, one his fate;
One showed sweet gifts from sweetest lands;
The other torn and empty hands.

At bird, and rose, and gem, and fruit,
The King was sad, the King was mute.
At last he slowly said: "My son
True treasure is not lightly won.

"Your brother's hands, wherein you see
Only these scars, show more to me
Than if a kingdom's price I found
In place of each forgotten wound."

# THE KING'S MEMENTO MORI.

INTO the regal face the risen sun
 Laughed, and he whispered in dismay:
"How is it, Victor of the World, that none
 Remind you what you are, to-day?

"Your sword shall teach the slave, who could forget
 That men are mortal, what they are!
How dared he sleep,—he has not warned me yet,—
 After that last, loth, lagging star?"

. . . Across his palace threshold, wan and still,
 His morning herald, wet with dew,
Stared at him with fixed eyes that well might chill
 The vanity of earth clean through.

"Good-morrow, King," he heard the dead lips say,
 "See what is man. When did I tell
My bitter message to my lord, I pray,
 So reverently and so well?"

# THE BROTHER'S HAND.

[TIME: THE CIVIL WAR, 1861-1868.]

HERE, see what I have brought you from the hill—
A brier-rose lingering late into July.
Oh, it may tell you, if it can and will,
 In its small way, so pink and timid, why
It waited after all its mates were dead,
And wore for mourning-garments only red
 While its step-mother month was fierce and dry.


There is no flower with look and bloom and breath,
 I fondly fancy, like the faint brier-rose ;
No flower so fair for life, so sweet for death,
 That in the dew or in the darkness grows ;
No flower that has so faërily heard and seen
What faëry things the hum and honey mean,
 When in the wind the bee about it blows.

Far off, by black-grey stone, in shattered heaps,
    The beautiful, familiar, sad home-grace,
Like love itself made palpable, it keeps
    Through all the sorrowful forsaken place.
Nor can you find the scented presence there,
On the green ground or in the pensive air,
    Of any other of the blossoming race.


A very lovely woman loved to wear
    Its cluster of blushes once upon her breast.
She brought it from the woods and set it where
    She always loved to be, herself, the best.
The very flowers we think so frail outstay
Our frailer selves—and she is gone away :
    Away—and, therefore, as we think, to rest.


On the seventh birthday of her fair twin-boys,
    She gave the two a boat, as they were one,
(For until then each owned the other's toys);
    But when they saw it floating in the sun,
With sails of stainéd silk so prettily blown,
Each felt that he was now himself alone:
    The golden chain that bound them was undone.

"No, it is mine," each to the other said,
   And one raised up an angry arm and made
A quick wide wound, that looked so strange and red
   Each of the other dimly felt afraid.
Then a child-Cain in shadowy terror stood,
And, crying from the ground, his brother's blood
   Rose from the pleasant shore where they had played.


That sharp, swift cut had cleft the two apart.
   And, under his light, lovely hair, one wore
A strange-shaped scar. And in the other's heart,
   A heart that had been very sweet before,
The snake-like passions started from their sleep
And over it began to writhe and creep.
   And so the two were two for evermore.


As they grew older, he who wore the scar
   Saw it was like a hand—his brother's hand,
It seemed, against him. Then he went afar
   With a kind kinsman to a colder land,
After he heard the dust begin to fall
On his young mother's coffin. She was all
   He had dear. And she was what the shadows are.

Blue-eyed and stately, with a bright, brave scorn
  Of wrong, he in a calmer climate grew.
The other, tropic-nursed as tropic-born,
  Was fierce and swarthy, and imperious too,
And restless as the wind that bloweth where
It listeth: so he wandered here and there.
  And neither of the other clearly knew.


At last there came a heavy hail of lead
  Out of the Northern sky, that Southward fell.
The fields were blasted and the men lay dead;
  The women moaned; and flying shapes of shell
Their ways from roof to hearth-stone madly tore,
And opened suddenly the deserted door,
  By the brier-roses guarded once so well.


And Ruin glided up the weedy path,
  And crossed the mouldy threshold and went in,
And sat there, with a sort of a sullen wrath,
  Gathering about her all that once had been
Dear and familiar—save the rose, beside
The crumbling porch, from which she vainly tried,
  Tearing her hands with thorns, the flowers to win.

And once, when a great ghastly Sight close by
    Was terrible in the stillness of the moon,
A tall, slight soldier, with a smothered cry,
    Crept close and broke some buds and vanished soon;
But, with an almost human joy-in-grief,
The desolate rose-tree thrilled from root to leaf
    When he said wearily : "Yes—it is I."


A whole year more, when summer flushed again,
    Near to the same place, in the glitter of heat,
(The earth was red, the sky was smoky then,)
    One lay in agony. Against his feet
A gashed and gory flag from its shot staff
Fluttered and fell. There was a cruel laugh
    From one he had not feared again to meet;


And a swift horse, deep-black, with foaming mouth
    And angry eyes full of wild wonder, sprung
From its light rider—one who loved the South
    With his whole bitter soul. And, as he flung
The reins away and stood in tears beside
The dying creature, gentle, till it died,
    He showed that he was desperate, dark, and young.

There was a beautiful and dreadful charm
About that youthful captain, as he stood
Bare-headed, swordless, with his dead right arm
Loose at his side, his left, whose strength was good,
About his horse—forgetting his own wound,
Forgetting all the horrible things around—
Calling it all the tender names he could.


But when his horse was gone, he turned away
And stamped the fallen flag and cursed, and shook
The tall, slight soldier in whose blood it lay,
Till he half-raised himself with a dim look,
That made the other loose his hateful hold
And tremble for an instant and grow cold,
As if his thought some deadly trouble took.


Then he crept closer to the wounded youth
And lifted, vaguely, his light lovely hair,
And that strange scar—the brother's hand, in truth
Against him—as in distant days was there.
But now that brother looked at his distress
With a remorse that changed to tenderness,
And tried to raise him with a timid care.

And watched him many a moaning after-night,
   Through which the shine of spectral steel would go,
Through which lost armies would rise up and fight
   Lost battles, in the air—then waver slow
And haze-like down, and whiten toward the dust,
Leaving behind a little blood and rust
   And glory. Glory ! Why, I do not know.


At last the War's fierce music left the wind,
   And they who answered to its infinite cries
With their whole breath were gone where God can find
   Them, when He searches land and sea and skies ·
And Peace remained—a beautiful white veil,
Wrought by hurt hands that dropped off thin and pale,
   To hide the tears in wan, wet, restless eyes.


And the twin-brothers—one just from his wound—
   Talked of their brier-rose that would blossom yet,
Talked of the river with its far-back sound,
   Talked of their mother with a still regret,
And of the fairy boat she gave them both :
And then a sudden silence showed them loth
   To talk of—what they did not quite forget.

Just then it happened that a pretty flash
　　Of small Spring-lightning made their window bright:
They saw a fluttering dress, a bright-plaid sash,
　　A wide straw-hat, and loose hair falling quite
Half-way to eager feet. And so they guessed,
Each in a shy half-dreaming way, the rest :
　　They thought the girl was lovely ? They were right.


Her face in glimpses came to haunt the two,
　　Her voice was not what common voices are ;
And soon the twin-born rivals darkly knew
　　The old feud was not dead. They saw the scar
Out of its dreary quiet rise again :
The brother's hand was terrible and plain
　　Against the brother, as in years afar.


She loved them both. Which most? I think that she—
　　At least not yet—nor any other knew.
Sometimes she walked with Frederick by the sea,
　　Sometimes she sung a tremulous song to Hugh,
And in a while, no doubt, began to know
That he was handsome, or she thought him so,
　　And that his eyes, perhaps, were frankly blue.

Out with the darker brother once, a storm
   Broke sharply down the twilight.   For a time
She clung to him.   But, dry again and warm,
   Among their lamps she sung a sobbing rhyme
To her piano—and the gold-haired man—
Whose desolate music ended and began
   With a far, subtle, creeping, sea-like chime.


Then hushed and went half-tearful to her room,
   Asking herself but this: "Which shall I choose?
Have I the saddest need of light or gloom?
   The fair one surely is too fair to lose:
Without him half the world were empty, and
Without his brother——if I understand,
   The dark one is too dark to quite refuse.


"And sometimes if I only glance at him,
   His richer, fiercer colour seems to me
To make his stiller brother look as dim
   As a star looks by lightning.   Let me be,
My star, with the white constant light you shed;
Fade out, my lightning, or else strike me dead.
   For star and lightning can but ill agree."

But something startled her brown window-bird,
　Nested below in perfume. As it flew
She heard her own name spoken, and she heard,
　Out in the wind, one ask: "Which of us two?
It is not well that both of us should stay.
Let her decide." In a bewildered way,
　Not knowing what she did, she whispered, "Hugh."


They heard below, and Frederick seemed to laugh,
　And said: "My boy, our paths again divide.
Your joy is great. If you could give me half,
　Enough were left. Good-bye. The world is wide,
But all too narrow to hold you and me.
Good-bye——and shall we let the Future be?
　Upon my faith you have a charming bride."


Next morning he was gone. And then, somehow,
　Hugh chanced in his vexed dreamy way to throw
The yellow hair from his unquiet brow,
　And started from a glass which seemed to show
That fearful scar, looking more deadly-white,
More like his brother's hand, too, since last night;
　Then scarlet suddenly it seemed to grow.

She saw it: "Ah, you have a scar," she said.
"How strange it is—and how much like a hand."
"It *is* a hand," he answered. "See how red
    It threatens now. It cut the gentle band
Between us while we yet were children." "Who?"
"We twins that called each other Fred and Hugh,
    And played beside a river in the sand."


A troubled paleness fell upon her face.
    She looked at him an instant. "If I may?"
She said, and, bird-like, fluttered from her place,
    And flushed and doubted, and—I must not say
She kissed the scar. But I can say it grew
Yet deeper scarlet, and looked darker too,
    And seemed to move—motioning her away.


. . . The leaf-bloom of the Autumn lit the woods—
    (The next day was to be their wedding-day).
A cruel rain whirled down in pitiless floods
    And fretted the poor leaves that tried to stay
And wear their splendour for a little yet.
The butterflies were faded out and wet,
    Or else the wind had blown them all away.

The crimson-curtained, pleasant parlour glowed
   With ferns and asters, and a sparkling fire;
The next-day's bride before the mirror showed
   The trailing mistiness of a bride's attire.
And Hugh looked at her, smiling from his dream:
He was not happy, quite, nor did he seem;
   Yet such sweet vanity he must admire.


She turned to take a letter that came in,
   And read it, and looked at him as she read,
And threw it at his feet. "And be your sin,"
   She hoarsely whispered, "upon your own head."
"My sin?" "See there, and—say it is not true."
"I will not. All I say is this: if you
   Believe it—let to-morrow not begin!"


Then there were angry words, and—"Let us part,"
   She moaned, and reached to him her frightened hand,
Thinking that he would hold it—to his heart—
   And kiss her pain away, as she had planned:
For she forgave him—what he had not done.
He answered: "As you please." And there was none
   To come between them, or to understand.

What then? The thistles blew across the rain,
  The grey, wet thorn-tree glimmered once and shook.
She thought: "If one should never come again—
  Should never come—after a bitter look?"
And—the dry asters from the mantel fell:
She brought no fresh ones for the vases. Well?
  And silence settled in his favourite book.


She did not thin her beauty with her tears,
  But was she tearless? Doubtless she was not.
But all the outward gladness of her years
  Was not because of one great grief forgot.
Loose hair and laughter, singing quick and sweet,
Followed about the green home-grass her feet,
  And quieted all wordless, kindly fears.


She had no mother. But her father said:
  "You are too hasty, little girl, I fear.
Hugh is a manly fellow; as for Fred——
  The villain! Hugh will come again, my dear,
Before the fashion of your dress shall change,
And we shall have our wedding." Was it strange?
  The dress grew quaint. And Hugh did not appear.

——Once at the sea-side, in an evening dance.
She felt—and, fluttering, tried to fly away—
The bird-like terror of the snake-like glance.
   Poor, charmèd little thing—and must it stay ?
" Frederick ? "   " Well—yes."   " Where is your
   brother, Hugh ? "
" Am I my brother's keeper ?   Doubtless you
   Who wounded and deserted him, can say."


Hurt and bewildered, then she brokenly tried
   The secret of his letter to recall.
His letter ?   With feigned anger he denied
   That he had written—anything at all !
" What a mysterious piece of villainy !
Hugh never could have thought so ill of me.
   He did not read it ? "   Then he heard her fall.


. . . It was the crowded room, and they must go
   Into the wide moonlighted air apart.
Where was his brother, then ?   He said, to know
   He would give up the last throb of his heart ;
It was two years or more since he had heard
Of Hugh one word, one single precious word :
   Then broke into a cry that made her start.

By dim degrees he made himself grow dear,
  By seeming everything his brother was.
Whatever in the other had been clear,
  In him she saw—darkly as in a glass.
At last, in some weird, subtle way, he grew
The shadow, or the very self, of Hugh.
  And—well, the Summer withered from the grass.


What then? The asters in the vases glowed
  Again; the parlour held the shining fire
Again; the mirror, three years older, showed
  The trailing mistiness of a bride's attire;
And, this time, Frederick watched her from his dream.
He was not happy, quite, nor did he seem,
  Yet such fair vanity he must admire.


Once more the thistles blew across the rain,
  The grey, wet thorn-tree glimmered once and shook;
And then she thought: "If one should come again—
  Or should not come—after a bitter look!"
And then—a sudden voice, familiar-low,
And phantom-sweet, but heavily-bent and slow,
  Read out the silence of the favourite book.

No matter. In a wedded year or two,
   In a far Western land a cottage rose,
With sand and sea and sea-shell shining through
   Its many windows—so the story goes.
Frederick was happy there. But his late bride
Had backward-yearning eyes, and sometimes sighed
   A little—as all women may ? Who knows ?


Once bitterly he asked : "What makes you sad ?"
   She answered languidly : "Perhaps the sea.
I sometimes think it surely has gone mad :
   It foams and mutters till it frightens me.
Sometimes when it looks only golden, and
All things look golden in this Golden Land,
   Blackly below it threatens things to be."


And, as her childish words failed at her lip,
   From silks and spices and a foreign sail,
She saw a man drop from a landing ship
   As heavily as he had been a bale
Of precious merchant-freight. With the great light
Of the great evening smitten, he was bright -
   But all who looked at him were dull and pale.

A lifeboat brought him strangling to the coast.
   He motioned them, in a despairing way,
To drown his body. For his soul was lost,
   He said: it shook him off and plûnged away
From the dark deck into the gulfs below,
For utter loneliness. And he must go
   And find it, somewhere—for the Judgment Day.


Then he died smiling. . . . Frederick and his wife
   Looked at him and each other, and then wound
Their arms about him. What was calm or strife
   To him or them? What had they lost and found?
What thing was near? What things were gone afar?
With tears, and without words, they kissed the scar—
   His brother's hand against him all his life.

# THE LAST ANGEL.

### A STORY TOLD OF CORREGGIO.

THE monks had shut his picture in, and,—yearning
   For one more last look, one, and yet one more,—
Heavily laden, with the hollows burning
   In his dusk cheek, he left the convent door.


Through the South sun he wandered homeward, moaning:
"His Christ for silver gave the Jew of old;
Have I not sinned like him beyond atoning?
   My Christ for copper I to-day have sold."


Alone he walked, afraid to meet the faces
   He loved the most on earth—Ah, bitter fate!
His beautiful starving children, with hot traces
   Of tears on cheeks, were crowded at the gate.

But one, the youngest, spent with innocent weeping
  Touched by the weird moon with a tender beam,
Among the shadows in the straw lay sleeping,
  Forgetting all, and laughing at her dream.

Her father looked at her and lifted slowly
  His dying hand : "Give me my brush," he said.
When his Last Angel, radiant and holy,
  Looked at him with his child's eyes, he was dead.

# DRAMATIC PERSONS AND MOODS.

## THE FANCY BALL.

As Morning you 'd have me rise
  On that shining world of art;
You forget: I have too much dark in my eyes—
  And too much dark in my heart.

"Then go as the Night—in June:
  Pass, dreamily, by the crowd,
With jewels to mock the stars and moon,
  And shadowy robes like cloud.

"Or as Spring, with a spray in your hair
  Of blossoms as yet unblown;
It will suit you well, for our youth should wear
  The bloom in the bud alone.

"Or drift from the outer gloom
  With the soft white silence of Snow:"
I should melt myself with the warm, close room—
  Or my own life's burning. No.

"Then fly through the glitter and mirth
  As a Bird of Paradise:"
Nay, the waters I drink have touched the earth;
  I breathe no summer of spice.

"Then——" Hush: if I go at all,
  (It will make them stare and shrink,
It will look so strange at a Fancy Ball)
  I will go as——Myself, I think!

---

## TWELVE HOURS APART.

He loved me. But he loved, likewise,
  This morning's world in bloom and wings;
Ah, does he love the world that lies
  In dampness, whispering shadowy things,
    Under this little band of moon?

He loves me? Will he fail to see
  A phantom hand has touched my hair
(And wavered, withering, over me)
  To leave a subtle greyness there,
    Below the outer shine of June?

He loves me ? Would he call it fair,
　The flushed half-flower he left me, say ?
For it has passed beneath the glare
　　And from my bosom drops away,
　　　Shaken into the grass with pain ?

He loves me ? Well, I do not know.
　A song in plumage crossed the hill
At sunrise when I felt him go—
　　And song and plumage now are still.
　　　He could not praise the bird again.

He loves me ? Veiled in mist I stand,
　My veins less high with life than when
To-day's thin dew was in the land,
　　Vaguely less beautiful than then—
　　　Myself a dimness with the dim.

He loves me ? I am faint with fear.
　He never saw me quite so old ;
I never met him quite so near
　　My grave, nor quite so pale and cold
　　　——Nor quite so sweet, he says, to him !

# A LILY OF THE NILE.

WHO was the beautiful woman whose lover
  Once left her this dead old flower, did you
    say ?
Well, perhaps that is she in the picture over
  The vase with the flowers which you gathered
    to-day.


The one with the deep strange dress, that is flowing
  All purple and pearls through each stiffened fold,
And the band on her forehead, whose dusk-red
    glowing
  Shoots into great sharp thorns of gold.


Never mind the light. You will see, to-morrow,
  That, with eyes raised darkly and lips close-
    prest,
She is giving away her awful sorrow
  To the snake she keeps at her breast !

"And who was her lover?"  Why, that may be he, there,
　In the other picture glimmering nigh—
Yes, the handsome and wretched man you see there,
　Falling against his sword to die.


Will he die for *her*, do you say?  (Ah, will he?)
　No doubt he has often told her so!
"Did it bloom far away, this crumbling lily?"
　Very far——and so long ago.


And who gave it to *me?*
　　　　　　　　——So the withered story
　I've dreamed by the twilight all this while,
For some vanished blossom's day of glory,
　Is your truth, my Lily of the Nile.


For the beautiful woman *is* slowly dying
　Of a snake as plain as this to my sight;
And her lover who gave her this flower is lying
　On the edge of a sword to-night.

# THERE WAS A ROSE.

"THERE was a rose," she said,
  "Like other roses, perhaps, to you.
Nine years ago it was faint and red,
  Away in the cold dark dew,
  On the dwarf bush where it grew.


"Never any rose before
  Was like that rose, very well I know;
Never another rose any more
  Will blow as that rose did blow,
  When the wet wind shook it so.


"What do I want?—Ah, what?
  Why, I want that rose, that wee one rose,
Only that rose. And that rose is not
  Anywhere just now? . . . God knows
  Where all the old sweetness goes.

"I want that rose so much;
I would take the world back there to the night
Where I saw it blush in the grass, to touch
It once in that Autumn light,
And only once, if I might.


"But a million marching men
From the North and the South would arise,
And the dead—would have to die again?
And the women's widowed cries
Would trouble anew the skies?


"No matter. I would not care;
Were it not better that this should be?
The sorrow of many the many bear,—
Mine is too heavy for me.
And I want that rose, you see!"

WASHINGTON, D. C., 1870.

## IF I WERE A QUEEN.

"But if you were a Queen?" you said.
   Well, then I think my favourite page
Should have a yellow, restless head,
   And be just your own pretty age.
So sweet in violet velvet, he
   Should tend my butterflies in herds,
Or help that belted knight, the bee,
   Win honey, or make little birds
Some little songs to sing for me—
              If I were a Queen.


A Queen—you saw one sitting by
   A tall man in a picture? Well.
He had a harp? You need not try—
   Her name is one you can not tell.
And so you wonder if I could
   Be Isolt, then? Not she, I fear,
To save Sir Tristram of the Wood
   And all his tripping silver deer;
For it were better to be good,
              If I were a Queen.

## IF I WERE A QUEEN.

Nor Guinevere —— You ask, would I
   Be Queen Elizabeth? Oh! no;
For, then, should I not have to die
   And leave, all hanging in a row,
Two thousand dresses? Could I bear
   To sit, majestic, cross, and grey,
With red paint on my nose, or wear,
   Down in my grave till Judgment Day,
The ring of Essex burning there,
           If I were a Queen?


Now let me ask myself awhile.
   Mary of Scotland, then?—since she
Haunts her grey castle with a smile
   That one man may have died to see:
She, fairest in Romance's light;
   She, saddest-storied of them all;
She—but it would not please me quite
   To climb a scaffold, or to fall
Beside my lovely head to-night,
           If I were a Queen.


Then she of Egypt—with the asp
   To drain my deadly beauty dry?—

To see my Roman lover clasp
  His sword with surer love, and die
Closer to it than me? Not so.
  No desert-snake with nursing grace
Should draw my fierce heart's fiercest glow;
  No coward of my conqueror's race
Should offer me his blood, I know—
        If I were a Queen.

Boädicéa? I were afraid
  To see her scythéd chariots shine!
—— Nor Vashti; for she disobeyed
  Her lord, the king in kingly wine!
Then she, the Queen of the East, who found
  The Wisest not so well arrayed,
In all his glory, as the ground
  Arrays its lilies?—Would I fade
Into some shrunken Bible mound,
        If I were a Queen?

Semiramis? Were it not sweet
  To have a palace mirror show [1]
How mad Assyria at my feet
  Might lie down like a lamb? And oh!

[1] Allusion to a celebrated painting of Semiramis.

To stand defiant, in the glare
   Of rising war, and softly say:
"My Beauty will subdue them!"   Rare
   And royal bloom must drop away;
Nor would I as a ghost look fair,
               If I were a Queen.


Penelopé?   No, on my word:
 · Vexed grievously with suitors, while
Much-wandering Ulysses heard
   Fine singing at the sirens' isle,
Too small were Ithaca for me!
   Then she whose gold hair glitters high
With stars caught in its tangles? [1]—See,
   How beautiful it is!   But I
Should choose my hair on Earth to be,
               If I were a Queen!


Nor slight, blonde Marie Antoinette?
   Nor she the Austrians called their King?
Nor any Blanche, or Margaret?
   Nor Russia's Catharine?   Would I bring
The Spanish woman's loth heart, then,
   From Aragon to England's throne?

[1] Berenice's hair.

Or be the Italian, widowed, when
 She, in a garret at Cologne,
Starved, a grey exile, shunned of men,
            If I were a Queen?

What Queen? Titania—since it seems
 A woman never quite can tire
Of kissing long, fair ears! In dreams
 My Gentle Joy I will admire,
And—but there is no Fairyland
 Left in the crowded world, no room
For dew, for anything but sand.
 Put out the moonshine, fold the bloom.
My feet could find no space to stand,
            If I were a Queen.

Ah! still I ask myself, what Queen?
 Well, one whose days were almost done,
Who felt her grave-grass turning green,
 Who saw the low light of the sun
Shrink from her palace windows, while
 Her whole court watched beside her bed,
Ready to say, without a smile:
"We loved the Queen. The Queen is dead."
Then they should grieve a little while,
            If I were a Queen.

And my whole court, I think, should show
  Three little heads of lightest gold,
Two others of a darker glow;
  And One bent low enough to hold
Between pale, quivering hands.  And then
  Some Silence should receive my soul,
My name should fade from lips of men,
  My pleasant funeral-bells should toll
This hour, and dust be dust again—
          If I were a Queen.

## SOMETIME.

WELL, either you or I,
  After whatever is to say is said,
Must see the other die,
  Or hear, through distance, of the other dead,
            Sometime.

And you or I must hide
  Poor empty eyes and faces, wan and wet
With Life's great grief, beside
  The other's coffin, sealed with silence, yet,
            Sometime.

And you or I must look
  Into the other's grave, or far or near,
And read, as in a book,
  Writ in the dust, words we made bitter here,
            Sometime.

Then, through what paths of dew,
  What flush of flowers, what glory in the grass,
Only one of us two,
  Even as a shadow walking, blind may pass,
            Sometime!

And, if the nestling song
  Break from the bosom of the bird for love,
No more to listen long
  One shall be deaf below, one deaf above,
            Sometime.

For both must lose the way
  Wherein we walk together, very soon:
One in the dusk shall stay,
  The other first shall see the rising moon,
            Sometime.

Oh! fast, fast friend of mine!
  Lift up the voice I love so much, and warn;—
To wring faint hands and pine,
  Tell me I may be left forlorn, forlorn,
            Sometime.

Say I may kiss through tears,
  For ever falling and for ever cold,
One ribbon from sweet years,
  One dear dead leaf, one precious ring of gold,
            Sometime.

Say you may think with pain
  Of some slight grace, some timid wish to please
Some eager look half vain
  Into your heart, some broken sobs like these,
            Sometime!

## THE ORDER FOR HER PORTRAIT.

I SAY what Cromwell said,
  (Smile, grey-haired sceptic, if you think me bold)
And that Italian count whose hair was red,—
  His great will would not have it painted gold.

No, I am brave, not vain;
  Braver than he of Macedon, since I
For Vanity's slight sake would hardly stain
  Art and the awful future with a lie:

You know that hand whose pride
  Within its hollow held one world, afar
Reaching for others, raised itself to hide
  On pictured brows the glory of a scar.

But paint me as I am,
  Whatever shape or colour you may see;
And do not fold the white fleece of the lamb
  About the yellow lioness, for me.

Ay, as I am. And then,
  No matter what you on your canvas find,
It shall not shrink before the eyes of men;
  It shall be truth—unless your soul be blind!

# THE CLOTHES OF A GHOST.

[*The Spirit of a beautiful and vain Woman speaks.*]

THEY were shut from me in a costly chest,
   Though I, in a woman's slight, sad way,
Of the lovely things that I loved the best,
   Held none, I fear me, so sweet as they—
        For I was daintily dressed.

A precious glimmer of gold was mine,
   To coil and charm on my bosom then;
And two great jewels whose restless shine
   Troubled the foolish hearts of men,
        Who fancied their light divine.

These thin hands wore on their tremulous grace
   Such fair little gloves as soft as snows;
And softly laid on this dim, fixed face
   Were calm, clear colours of white and rose,
        In another time and place.

## THE CLOTHES OF A GHOST.

There's a withering, weird half-picture of me—
    No, of my clothes—on a shadowy wall:
A wonderful painter, they said, was he,
    Who studied my drapery, that was all,
        Not guessing what I might be.

Yet he followed me, in my far, flushed day,
    And thought he knew me, and held me dear;
And now, should I waver across his way,
    He would grow as ghastly as I am, with fear,
        Though he is so wise and grey!

But my beautiful clothes were his despair—
    They were so well-cut, so charmingly made.
It is best that they were not worn threadbare;
    It is best that I did not feel them fade;
        It is best—did *he* ever care?

I, a thing too fearfully fine to show,
    Or stain the starlight wherein I pass,
Must still have the old, fierce vanity grow,
    Must yearn by the water, as by a glass,
        For a glimpse of—nothing, I know!

Oh, my lovely clothes that I still admire!
    They were only fashioned for moth and rust;

Yet I, their wearer, though scarred by fire,
  Shall sit with the gentle ghosts, I trust,
      Who once wore meaner attire!

For, had I been less like the lilies arrayed—
  They of the field that toil not nor spin—
I had thought of my Father's work, nor stayed
  In empty glory, in shining sin,
      Far into the final shade.

## FLIGHT.

THROUGH field and flood and fire I go,—
Wherefore and where I do not know.

Through field,—my tangled path is crossed
With winds and stinging spears of frost.

Through field,—the stones rise up and wound
My fearful feet, that stain the ground.

Through field,—sometimes one rose forlorn
Gives me its flush, without its thorn.

Through flood,—the wide rains beat my brow
The world is only water now.

Through flood,—wave after wave there is:
Wave after wave,—what else but this?

Through flood,—one sea another meets;
See Arctic ice in tropic heats!

Through flood,—there is one ship in sight:
If I might reach it,—if I might!

Through fire,—what flames and flames there be!
The world is only fire to me.

Through fire,—how palace spire and wall
Put shining garments on and fall!

Through fire,—I hear the last voice cry,
"The world is ashes." But am I?

Calm on the awful element,
I turn and say, "I am content."

## MARBLE OR DUST?

A CHILD, beside a statue, said to me,
    With pretty wisdom very sadly just,
"That man is Mr. Lincoln, Mama. He
    Was made of marble; we are made of dust."

One flash of passionate sorrow trembled through
    The dust of which I had been dimly made,
One fierce, quick wish to be of marble too—
    Not something meaner, that must fall and fade.

"To be for ever fair and still and cold,"
    I faintly thought, with faint tears in my sight;
"To stand thus face to face with Time, and hold
    Between us that uncrumbling charm of white;

"To see the creatures formed of slighter stuff
    Waver in little dead-leaf whirls away,
Yet know that I could wait and have enough
    Of frost and dew, enough of dark and day.

... "I would be marble? Wherefore? Just to
   miss
The tremors of glad pain that dust must know?—
The grief that settles after some dead kiss?—
The frown that was a smile not long ago?

"Do I forget the stone's long loneliness?—
   The dumb impatience all wan watching brings?—
The looking with blind eyes, in vague distress,
   For Christ's slow Coming and the End of Things?

"No, boy of mine, with your young yellow hair,
   Better the dust you scatter with your feet
Than marble, which can see not you are fair—
   Than marble, which can feel not you are sweet.

"Ay, or than marble which must meet the years
   Without my light relief of murmurous breath;
Without the bitter sweetness of my tears—
   Without the love which dust must have for Death."

## THEIR LOST PICTURE.

"No, it was nothing old and grand :
  Only a child, out in the sun,
Choking a kitten with one hand,
  And crushing pretty flowers with one.

"Some rosebuds, sweet as buds could be,
  Were blown against the blowing hair;
The clear eyes watched a cedar-tree,
  That held a red-bird flaming there.

"The frame around was dark and small.
  Just opposite the open door,
One morning, on our cottage wall
  It hung, when we were young and poor.

"This little piece of light and bloom
  Was more, a thousand times, to me
Than all you have seen in great church-gloom,
  Or palace-gallery light, could be.

"——You do not understand, I say.
  We saw the picture in the glass,
In our first home so far away,
  When our dead child played in the grass"

# THE PALACE-BURNER.

## [PARIS, 1871.]

*A Picture in a Newspaper.*

SHE has been burning palaces. "To see
   The sparks look pretty in the wind?" Well, yes—
And something more. But women brave as she
   Leave much for cowards, such as I, to guess.

But this is old, so old that everything
   Is ashes here—the woman and the rest.
Two years are—oh! so long. Now you may bring
   Some newer pictures.—You like this one best?

You wish that you had lived in Paris then?
   You would have loved to burn a palace, too?
But they had guns in France, and Christian men
   Shot wicked little Communists like you.

You would have burned the palace?—Just because
   You did not live in it yourself! Oh! why
Have I not taught you to respect the laws?
   *You* would have burned the palace—would not *I*?

## THE PALACE-BURNER.

Would I? . . . Go to your play. . . . Would I,
    indeed?
  *I?* Does the boy not know my soul to be
Languid and worldly, with a dainty need
    For light and music? Yet he questions me.

Can he have seen my soul more near than I?
    Ah! in the dusk and distance sweet she seems,
With lips to kiss away a baby's cry,
    Hands fit for flowers, and eyes for tears and
    dreams.

Can he have seen my soul? And could she wear
    Such utter life upon a dying face:
Such unappealing, beautiful despair:
    Such garments—soon to be a shroud—with grace?

Would *I* burn palaces? The child has seen
    In this fierce creature of the Commune here,
So bright with bitterness and so serene,
    A being finer than my soul, I fear.

# A MASKED BALL.

There, in the music strangely met,
   From lands and ages wide apart,
They came, like ghosts remembering yet
   The old sweet yearning of the heart.

What sad and shining names were heard!
   What stories swept the dust, like trains!
What minster-buried echoes stirred!
   What backward splendours, backward stains!

Still two by two, as moved by fate,
   They came from silence and from song;
The tyranny of love or hate
   With that mock-pageant passed along.

There kings and cardinals long gone
   Forgot their feuds, and joined the dance.
His Holiness himself looked on,
   With something merry in his glance.

There, priestly, yet not loth to please,
   Stood Abelard; by some sad whim,
In convent coif, poor Héloïse
   Was near, confessing—what?—to him.

There, with forlornest beauty wan,
    Young Amy Robsart walked unseen,
While my Lord Leicester's looks were on
    Elizabeth, his gracious queen.


There—though the blonde Rowena gazed,
    Gold-haired and stately, with surprise—
Jewelled and dark, Rebecca raised
    The Saxon knight half-wistful eyes.


And there, despite his inky cloak,
    The melancholy Dane seemed gay,
And to Polonius' daughter spoke
    Things Shakespeare does not have him say.


"I think," he said, "I know you by
    That most fantastic wreath you wear."
She, with a little languid sigh,
    Asked—if his father's ghost were there.


"That voice—though veiled, it can not hide.
    One trifling favour I would ask:
Give me—Yourself." "No, no," she cried;
    "You are—a stranger in a mask."

What more ?  Ah, well!  Ophelia fled
From Hamlet—when his mask was raised.
"I—was—mistaken," Hamlet said,
As in Ophelia's face he gazed.


Ah, in the world, as at the ball,
　There is a mask that lovers wear;
We call it Youth.  But let it fall,
　Then,—Hamlet and Ophelia stare.

---

## A DOUBT.

IT is subtle, and weary, and wide;
It measures the world at my side;
　It touches the stars and the sun;
It creeps with the dew to my feet;
　It broods on the blossoms, and none,
Because of its brooding, are sweet;
It slides as a snake in the grass,
Whenever, wherever I pass.

## A DOUBT.

It is blown to the South with the bird;
At the North, through the snow, it is heard;
   With the moon from the chasms of night
It rises, forlorn and afraid;
   If I turn to the left or the right
I can not forget or evade;
When it shakes at my sleep as a dream,
If I shudder, it stifles my scream.

It smiles from the cradle; it lies
On the dust of the grave, and it cries
   In the winds and the waters; it slips
In the flush of the leaf to the ground;
   It troubles the kiss at my lips;
It lends to my laughter a sound;
It makes of the picture but paint;
It unhaloes the brow of the saint.

The ermine and crown of the king,
The sword of the soldier, the ring
   Of the bride, and the robe of the priest,
The gods in their prisons of stone,
   The angels that sang in the East—
Yea, the cross of my Lord, it has known;
And wings there are none that can fly
From its shadow with me, till I die!

# A WOMAN'S BIRTHDAY.

[IN AUGUST.]

It is the Summer's great last heat,
It is the Fall's first chill: they meet.
Dust in the grass, dust in the air,
Dust in the grave—and everywhere!
Ah, late rose, eaten to the heart:
Ah, bird, whose southward yearnings start:
The one may fall, the other fly.
Why may not I? Why may not I?


Oh, Life! that gave me for my dower
The hushing song, the worm-gnawed flower,
Let drop the rose from your shrunk breast
And blow the bird to some warm nest;
Flush out your dying colours fast:
The last dead leaf—will be the last.
No? Must I wear your piteous smile
A little while, a little while?

## A WOMAN'S BIRTHDAY.

The withering world accepts her fate
Of mist and moaning, soon or late;
She had the dew, the scent, the spring
And upward rapture of the wing;
Their time is gone, and with it they.
And am I wooing Youth to stay
In these dry days, that still would be
Not fair to me, not fair to me?


If Time has stained with gold the hair,
Should he not gather greyness there?
Whatever gifts he chose to make,
If he has given, shall he not take?
His hollow hand has room for all
The beauty of the world to fall
Therein. I give my little part
With aching heart, with aching heart.

## COMFORT—BY A COFFIN.

Ah, friend of mine,
The old enchanted story!—Oh,
I cannot hear a word!
Tell some poor child who loved a bird,
And knows he holds it stained and still,
"It flies—in Fairyland!
Its nest is in a palm-tree, on a hill;
Go, catch it—if you will!"

Ah, friend of mine,
The music (which ear hath not heard?)
At best wails from the skies,
Somehow, into our funeral cries!
The flowers (eye hath not seen?) still fail
To hide the coffin lid;
Against this face, so pitiless now and pale,
Can the high heavens avail?

Ah, friend of mine,
I think you mean—to mean it all!
But then an angel's wing
Is a remote and subtle thing,

(If you could show me any such
 In air that I can breathe !)
And surely Death's cold hand has much, so much,
 About it we can touch !


Ah, friend of mine,
Say nothing of the thorns—and then
 Say nothing of the snow.
God's will ?  It is—that thorns must grow,
Despite our bare and troubled feet,
 To crown Christ on the cross :
The snow keeps white watch on the unrisen wheat;
 And yet—the world is sweet.


Ah, friend of mine,
I know, I know—all you can know !
 All you can say is—this :
"It is the last time you can kiss
This only one of all the dead,
 Knowing it is the last;
These are the last tears you can ever shed
 On this fair fallen head."

## WE TWO.

God's will is—the bud of the rose for your hair,
    The ring for your hand and the pearl for your
        breast;
God's will is—the mirror that makes you look fair.
    No wonder you whisper: "God's will is the best."

But what if God's will were the famine, the flood?—
    And were God's will the coffin shut down in your
        face?—
And were God's will the worm in the fold of the bud,
    Instead of the picture, the light, and the lace?

Were God's will the arrow that flieth by night,
    Were God's will the pestilence walking by day,
The clod in the valley, the rock on the height—
    I fancy "God's will" would be harder to say.

God's will is—your own will. What honour have you
    For having your own will, awake or asleep?
Who praises the lily for keeping the dew,
    When the dew is so sweet for the lily to keep?

God's will unto me is not music or wine.
With helpless reproaching, with desolate tears,
God's will I resist, for God's will is divine;
And I—shall be dust to the end of my years.

God's will is—not mine. Yet one night I shall lie
Very still at his feet, where the stars may not shine.
"Lo! I am well pleased," I shall hear from the sky;
Because—it is God's will I do, and not mine.


## ENCHANTED.

She sat in a piteous hut,
   In a wood where poisons grew.
Withered was every leaf,
   And her face was withered too.
Like a sword the sharp wind cut
   Her worn heart through and through.

Away, and so far away,
   She looked for a light and a sign:
"Oh, he has not forgotten me!
   What should I care for to-day,
When all to-morrow is mine?
   I am content to stay."

## ENCHANTED.

On the heights the hail would beat,
  In the thorns would sink the snow,
And the chasms were weird with sound;
  Yet the years would come and go:
"Somewhere there is something sweet,
  And some time I shall know.

"There is a land close by,
  A land in reach of my arm;
It is mine from shore to sea;—
  There the nightingales do fly,
There the flush of the rose is warm:
  I shall take it by and by.

"But the shape that guards the gate,
  Where my mirror waits to show
How beautiful I am,
  Oh, he makes me loth to go.
I wait, and I wait, and I wait,—
  Through fear of him, I know.

"But who breaks this charm of breath
  Enchantment himself must wear.
Two from each other shrink
  In the freezing dark, and stare: . . .
Your kiss for my kiss, O Death!
  Each makes the other fair."

# THE ALTAR AT ATHENS.

["TO THE UNKNOWN GOD."]

BECAUSE my life was hollow with a pain
   As old as—death: because my eyes were dry
As the fierce tropics after months of rain:
   Because my restless voice said "Why?" and
     "Why?"

Wounded and worn, I knelt within the night,
   As blind as darkness—Praying? And to Whom?—
When yon cold crescent cut my folded sight,
   And showed a phantom Altar in my room.

It was the Altar Paul at Athens saw.
   The Greek bowed there, but not the Greek alone;
The ghosts of nations gathered, wan with awe,
   And laid their offerings on that shadowy stone.

The Egyptian worshipped there the crocodile,
   There they of Nineveh the bull with wings;
The Persian there, with swart sun-lifted smile,
   Felt in his soul the writhing fire's bright stings.

There the weird Druid held his mistletoe;
　There for the scorched son of the sand, coiled bright,
The torrid snake was hissing sharp and low;
　And there the Atlantic savage paid his rite.

"Allah!" the Moslem darkly muttered there;
　"Brahma!" the jewelled Indies of the East
Sighed through their spices, with a languid prayer;
　"Christ?" faintly questioned many a paler priest.

And still the Athenian Altar's glimmering Doubt
　On all religions—evermore the same.
What tears shall wash its sad inscription out?
　What Hand shall write thereon His other name?


## HER CROSS AND MINE.

"This is my cross—here, Sister, see:
　The only one I have to bear."
A flash of gold fell over me,
　And precious lights were everywhere.

## HER CROSS AND MINE.

She was a lovely, restless thing,
   With time in blossom at her feet,
And on her hand the enchanted ring
   Whose promise always is so sweet.

I was a nun. My fearless eyes
   Had looked their last on youth. I guessed
At something quiet in the skies,
   And veiled my face against the rest.

My cross was dark and darkly stained,
   Even from the heart of one who died :—
Invisible drops of blood had rained
   Thereon, when love was crucified.

That laughing girl could pity me,
   Because she fancied from my cross
The world had fallen. Such as she
   Still think to lose the world—is loss !

Yet, heavier is her cross than mine,
   For in the fatal jewels there
(Oh, will she ask for help divine ?)
   I know she has the world to bear.

## TWO IN TWO WORLDS.

A PEASANT girl sat in the grass,
　　With just a peasant's eyes to see
The king's fair son when he should pass;—
　　From farthest Fairyland was he.

" He cannot love me—but he might,
　　If this or that had chanced to be.
It breaks my heart to know how slight
　　The things that hold him high from me.

"Had I been born in yonder tower,
　　With just a jewel for my hair,—
Not half so sweet as this one flower,—
　　He would have climbed to reach me there.

"Just for some fairness in my face;
　　Some ermine on a train of state;
Some poor, dead name that he could trace
　　To royal tombs—I were his mate!

"So brief the distance then between
　Palace and hut, need I be sad?—
Almost he loves me.  Ay, a queen
　I were—if but a crown I had!


"Ah me, unhappy in my place!
　What matter, since they are apart,
Whether one rose-leaf or all space
　Divide divided heart and heart?"


. . . It was a thousand years ago.
　To-night Time tells the tale anew:
I am that peasant girl, I know;
　And, sir, the king's fair son are you!

# CAPRICE AT HOME.

No, I will not say good-bye—
Not good-bye, nor anything.
He is gone. . . . I wonder why
   Lilacs are not sweet this spring.
   How that tiresome bird will sing!


I might follow him and say
   Just that he forgot to kiss
Baby, when he went away.
   Everything I want I miss.
   Oh, a precious world is this!


. . . What if night came and not he?
   Something might mislead his feet.
Does the moon rise late? Ah me!
   There are things that he might meet.
   Now the rain begins to beat:

So it will be dark. The bell?—
  Some one some one loves is dead.
Were it he——! I cannot tell
  Half the fretful words I said,
  Half the fretful tears I shed.


Dead? And but to think of death!—
  Men might bring him through the gate:
Lips that have not any breath,
  Eyes that stare——And I must wait!
  Is it time, or is it late?


I was wrong, and wrong, and wrong;
  I will tell him, oh, be sure!
If the heavens are builded strong,
  Love shall therein be secure;
  Love like mine shall there endure.


. . . Listen, listen—that is he!
  I'll not speak to him, I say.
If he choose to say to me,
  "I was all to blame to-day;
  Sweet, forgive me," why—I may!

# A WALL BETWEEN.

*[A piteous thing, you know,*
*Half hinted, at the edge of the earth, my friend:*
*Clinging to its last clod, She whispers low,*
*Not knowing He has listened till the end.*
*A woman's tale (of wrong and grief),*
*And, therefore, none too brief.*

*He who could leave her heart,*
*Spite of youth's passionate promises, to break*
*(While through their children's home he walked, apart,*
*Dumb as the dead), must, for her soul's sweet sake,*
*Come, at the last, in priest-disguise*
*To help her to the skies !]*

THEN, do I doubt ? Not so.
Though the stars wander without any Guide
Out there in loneliest dark, almost I know—
I do believe that He was crucified.
Arisen and ascended to
The Heaven ? Oh, priest, I do.

Still, you were kind to come.
Only to tell me, then, that I must die ?
I knew as much. Ah me, the mouth was dumb

That told me first (let bygone things go by),—
    The young sad mouth, without a breath.
    Yes, I believe in death.

    (A crucifix to kiss?)
Another world may light your lifted eyes,
    But, by my heart that breaks, I am of this.
Are you quite sure those palms of Paradise
    Do shelter for me one sweet head?
    Or, are the dead—the dead?

    It is a vain world? Oh,
It is a goodly world,—a world wherein
    We hear the doves (that moan?)—the winds (that blow
The buds away?) It is a world of sin,
    And therefore sorrow?—Was it, then,
    Fashioned and formed of men?

    Pray, would you give one rood
Of your dark, certain soil, where olives grow,
    For all those shining heights on heights, where brood
The wings you babble of that shame the snow?
    —— Why, what new song? But I have heard
    In our own trees a bird.

(Oh, call it what you will!)
Light, hollow, brief, and bitter? Yes, I know.
>With cruel seas and sands? Yes, yes, and
still——
And fire and famine following where we go?
>And still I leave it at my feet,
>Moaning, "The world is sweet."

>Why, it was here that I
Had youth and all that only youth can bring.
>Fair sir, if you would help a woman die,
Show me a glass. There! that one look will wring
>My heart, I think, out of its place;—
>The earth may take my face.

>Think of the blessèd skies?
If in the cheek one have no rose to wear,
>If nights all full of tears have changed the eyes,—
Why, would one be immortal and not fair?
>With faded hair, one would not quite
>Contrast an aureole's light.

>You talk of things unseen
With all the pretty arrogance of a boy.
>Why, one could laugh at what you think you
>mean.

## A WALL BETWEEN.

You see the bud upon the bough with joy,
    You look through summer toward the fruit——
        The worm is at the root?


    Well—if it is. You see,
Your feet are set among our pleasant dews;
    Therefore, that crown of phantom stars for me,
In distance most divine, you kindly choose,
        Content to leave your own unwon,
        And shine here with the sun.


    Hush! Wait! Somehow—I know.
You do remind me tenderly of—yes,
    Of him, your kinsman (long, so long ago),
But for these sacred garments. I confess,
        Oh, father, I cannot forget
        The world where he stays yet!


    Quick! will you look away?
Too cruelly like him in the dusk you grow,—
    This awful dusk that ends it all, I say.
You pity us when we are young, you know,
        And lose a lover. Surely then
        There may be other men.

But when the hand we bind
So that it cannot reach out anywhere,
    Then find, or, sadder, fancy that we find,
The ring is not true gold, you do not care;—
    These tragedies writ in wedding rings
    Are common, tiresome things.


    On earth there was one man,—
There were no men. They all had faded through
    His shadow. Surely, where our grief began,
In that old garden, he, that one of two,
    Looked not to Eve, before the Fall,
    So much the lord of all.


    And yet he said——I crave
Your patience. I will not forget to die.
    And there is no remembrance in the grave;
That comforts one. Better it is to lie
    Not knowing thistles grow above,
    Than to remember love.


    . . . Now you may call my friends,—
Ah, my sweet friends. They whispered just a word
    Or two last night here by me. To what ends

They look through tears! I thank them that I heard.
    "A charming chance," one lightly said;
        The other's cheek burned red.


    The blush I could not see
I felt, like fire. Then they both laughed,—and this
    Beside the dying. He, they said, would be
Handsome and lonely. Lonely? Will he miss
    The flower they bury in my breast,
        Up here with all the rest?


    Yes, we have many a year,
And then we have one hour—and he away!
    Why, there was something only he should hear.
. . . He wore his cloak?—it is so cold for May.
    ——If he would come (the lamp looks dim),
        I'd leave the world—to him.


    Then tell him, priest, if he——
Tell him, I pray you, this—ah, yet he said——
    Then only tell him—nothing sweet for me.
Tell him I have not tasted once his bread
    Since then. Tell him I die too proud
        To take of him a shroud.

## A WALL BETWEEN.

  I, with the raven's trust
For food, the lily's trust for raiment, found
  Who feeds the one and clothes the other must
Remember me. My hands, through many a wound,
  That which they had were glad to earn.
  He gave—what I'll return.


  Ask him if I forgot
One household care. If I, in such poor ways
  As I could know, through piteous things have not
Tried still to please him, lo, these many days;—
  Ah, bitter task, self-set and vain!
  ——I hear the wind and rain.


  I fear he will be wet,
And—not afraid—but, somehow, something might
  Trouble him in the dark. You know he met
Strange men, somewhere, he said, one lonesome night.
  If anything should hurt him, I—
  Yes, I forgot—could die.


  I have not seen his face
Since then. We lived a wall apart, we two,
  While dark and void between us was all space.

Sometimes I hid, and watched his shadow through
    Too wistful eyes, as it would pass,
        Ghost-like, from off the grass.


Tell him, beneath his roof
I felt I had not where to lay my head,
    Yet could not dare the saintly world's reproof,
And withered under my own scorn instead;
    Still whispering, "For the children's sake,"
        I let my slow heart break.


The children? Let them sleep—
To waken motherless. Could I put by
    Their arms, and lie like snow, and have them weep,
With my own eyes so empty and so dry?
    I've left some pretty things, you see,
        To comfort them for me,—


Sweet dresses, curious toys——
But, after all, what will the baby do?
    . . . Hush! Here he is, waked by the wind's
        wild noise.
Let mother count the dimples, one and two.
    Whose baby has the goldenest head?
        I dreamed once he was dead.

Dead, and for many a year?—
Can a dead baby laugh and babble so?
Do you not see me kiss and kiss him here,
And hold death from me still to kiss him?—No?
Yet I did dream white blossoms grew——
Do cruel dreams come true?


. . . As the tree falls, one says,
So shall it lie.  It falls, remembering
The sun and stillness of its leaf-green days,
The moons it held, the nested bird's warm wing,
The promise of the buds it wore,
The fruit—it never bore.


So, take my cross, and go.
Where my Lord Christ descended I descend.
Shall I ascend like Him?—I do not know.
I loved the world; the world is at an end.
Therefore, I pray you, shut your book,
And take away that look.


That look—of his!  You stay.
Then, say I loved him bitterly to the last!
Who loves one sweetly loves not much, I say.

## A WALL BETWEEN. 107

Love's blush by moonlight will fade out full fast.
Love's lightning scar at least we keep.
Now, let me—go to sleep.

. . . His voice, too, in disguise!
It is—in pity, no! Yes, it is *he!*—
With tears of memory in his steadfast eyes.
Mock-priest, how sharply you have shriven me!
Your cousin's righteous robes——I fear
You had somewhat to hear.

Ah?——Had you said but this
A year ago. Now, let my chill hand fall;
It gives you back your youth.—But you will miss
My shadow from your sunshine. That is all
Yet—if some lovelier life shall dawn
And I should love you on?

Good-bye. Was it well done?
You know that Eastern tale, where gifts of gold
And glory—as a king's comfort—came to one
Who, having starved, went out with courtesy cold
To meet and waive that bitter state,
Dumbly, through his own gate.

## A LESSON IN A PICTURE.

So it is whispered here and there,
   That you are rather pretty? Well?
(Here's matter for a bird of the air
   To drop down from the dusk and tell.)
Let's have no lights, my child. Somehow,
The shadow suits your blushes now.

The blonde young man who called to-day
   (He only rang to leave a book?—
Yes, and a flower or two, I say!)
   Was handsome, look you. Will you look?
You did not know his eyes were fine?
You did not! Can you look in mine?

What is it in this picture here,
   That you should suddenly watch it so?
A maiden leaning half in fear,
   From her far casement; and, below,
In cap and plumes (or cap and bells?)
Some fairy tale her lover tells.

Suppose this lonesome night could be
   Some night a thousand springs ago,
Dim round that tower; and you were she,
   And your shy friend her lover (Oh!),
And I—her mother! And suppose
I knew just why she wore that rose.


Do you think I'd kiss my girl, and say:
   "Make haste to bid the wedding guest,
And make the wedding garment gay,—
   You could not find in East or West
So brave a bridegroom; I rejoice
That you have made so sweet a choice"?


Or say, "To look for ever fair,
   Just keep this turret moonlight wound
About your face; stay in mid-air;—
   Rope-ladders lead one to the ground,
Where all things take the touch of tears,
And nothing lasts a thousand years"?

## FROM TWO WINDOWS.

He was young—and he saw the South:
  The bird and the rose were there,
And the god with the lifted look
  And the laurel in his hair.
Before him a palace stood;—
  A shy wind moved the lace,
And showed by the light of a dream
  A woman's wonderful face.

He was old—and he saw the North:
  The mountains were fierce and bare,
And pitiless swords of ice
  Were thrust at him from the air.
A ruin blackened the moon;
  And in that forlornest place,
Wasted with famine and tears,
  Lo, a woman's dreadful face!

# DENIED.

## I.

[THE LADY'S THOUGHT.]

IT may have been——Who knows, who knows?
   It was too dark for me to see.
The wind that spared this very rose
   Its few last leaves could hardly be
     Sadder of voice than he.

A foreign Prince here in disguise,
   Who asked a shelter from the rain:
(The country that he came from lies
   Above the clouds.) He asked in vain
     And will not come again.

If I *had* known that it was He
   Who had not where to lay His head:—
"But my Lord Christ, it cannot be;
   My guest-room has too white a bed
     For wayside dust," I had said.

## II.

[THE MOTHER'S THOUGHT.]

IT was my own sweet child—the one
  Whose baby mouth breathes at my breast.
(A fairer and a brighter none,
  Save His own Mother, ever prest
    Into diviner rest.)

He had escaped my arms and strayed
  Into the pitiless world that night.
With wounded feet and faith betrayed,
  Charmed backward by a glimmer of light,
    Almost he stood in sight.

Oh, I had let *him* ask in vain,
  (Vague, lonesome, shadowy years ahead,)
My roof to hide him from the rain,
  My lamp to comfort him, my bread,
    Who came as from the dead!

## AFTER THE QUARREL.

Hush, my pretty one. Not yet.
   Wait a little, only wait.
Other blue flowers are as wet
   As your eyes, outside the gate
He has shut for ever.—But
*Is* the gate for ever shut?

Just a young man in the rain
   Saying (the last time?) "good-night!"
*Should* he never come again
   Would the world be ended quite?
Where would all these rosebuds go?—
All these robins? Do you know?

But—he will not come? Why, then,
   Is no other within call?
There are men, and men, and men—
   And these men are brothers all!
Each sweet fault of his you'll find
Just as sweet in all his kind.

None with eyes like his ? Oh—oh !
   In diviner ones did I
Look, perhaps, an hour ago.
   Whose ? Indeed (you must not cry)
Those I thought of—are not free
   To laugh down your tears, you see.

Voice like his was never heard ?
   No—but better ones, I vow ;
Did you ever hear a bird ?—
   Listen, one is singing now !
And his gloves ? His gloves ? Ah, well,
   There are gloves like his to sell.

At the play to-night you'll see,
   In mock-velvet cloaks, mock earls
With mock-jewelled swords, that he
   Were a clown by !—Now, those curls
Are the barber's pride, I say ;
   Do not cry for them, I pray.

If no one should love you ? Why,
   You can love some other still :
Philip Sidney, Shakespeare, ay,
   Good King Arthur, if you will ;
Raphael—*he* was handsome too.
   Love them one and all. I do.

# THE DESCENT OF THE ANGEL.

"THIS is the house. Come, take the keys,
   Romance and Travel here must end."
Out of the clouds, not quite at ease,
   I saw the pretty bride descend;—
With satin sandals, fit alone
To glide in air, she touched the stone.

A thing to fade through wedding lace,
   From silk and scents, with priest and ring,
Floated across that earthly place
   Where life must be an earthly thing.
An earthly voice was in her ears,
Her eyes awoke to earthly tears.

# DOUBLE QUATRAINS.

### I.

#### "WE WOMEN."

HEART-ACHE and heart-break—always that or this.
  Sometimes it rains just when the sun should shine;
Sometimes a glove or ribbon goes amiss;
  Sometimes, in youth, your lover should be mine.

Still madam frets at life, through pearls and lace
  (A breath can break her pale heart's measured beat),
And still demands the maid who paints her face
  Shall find the world for ever smooth and sweet.

### II.

#### WORD OF COUNSEL.

OTHERS will kiss you while your mouth is red.
  Beauty is brief. Of all the guests who come
While the lamp shines on flowers, and wine, and bread,
  In time of famine who will spare a crumb?

## DOUBLE QUATRAINS. 117

Therefore, oh, next to God, I pray you keep
  Yourself as your own friend, the tried, the true.
Sit your own watch—others will surely sleep.
  Weep your own tears. Ask none to die with you.

### III.

#### BROKEN PROMISE.

AFTER strange stars, inscrutable, on high;
  After strange seas beneath his floating feet;
After the glare in many a brooding eye,—
  I wonder if the cry of "Land" was sweet?

Or did the Atlantic gold, the Atlantic palm,
  The Atlantic bird and flower, seem poor, at best,
To the grey Admiral under sun and calm,
  After the passionate doubt and faith of quest?

### IV.

#### UTTER DARKNESS.

IF I should have void darkness in my eyes
  While there were violets in the sun to see;
If I should fail to hear my child's sweet cries,
  Or any bird's voice in our threshold tree;

If I should cease to answer love or wit:
Blind, deaf, or dumb, how bitter each must be!
Blind, deaf, or dumb—I will not think of it!
. . . Yet the night comes when I shall be all three.

V.

THE HAPPIER GIFT.

DIVINEST words that ever singer said
Would hardly lend your mouth a sweeter red;
Her aureole, even hers whose book you hold,
Could give your head no goldener charm of gold.

Ah me! you have the only gift on earth
That to a woman can be surely worth
Breathing the breath of life for. Keep your place
Even she had given her fame to have your face.

VI.

IN DOUBT.

THROUGH dream and dusk a frightened whisper said:
"Lay down the world: the one you love is dead."
   In the near waters, without any cry
   I sank, therefore—glad, oh so glad, to die!

Far on the shore, with sun, and dove, and dew,
And apple-flowers, I suddenly saw you.
   Then—was it kind or cruel that the sea
   Held back my hands, and kissed and clung to me?

### VII.

#### A LOOK INTO THE GRAVE.

I LOOK, through tears, into the dust to find
   What manner of rest man's only rest may be.
The darkness rises up and smites me blind.
   The darkness—is there nothing more to see?

Oh, after flood, and fire, and famine, and
   The hollow watches we are made to keep
In our forced marches over sea and land—
   I wish we had a sweeter place to sleep.

### VIII.

#### ETIQUETTE.

IN some old Spanish court there chanced to be
   No one whose office was to save the king
From death by fire. The king himself? Not he;—
   Could royal hands have done so mean a thing?

My boy, through life think how this king of Spain
  (Whose name none knows—and so you'll not
    forget!)
Caught by his palace hearth-flames, not in vain
  To ashes burned—for sake of Etiquette!


IX.

SEPTEMBER.

SEND back these lonesome lights to Fairyland,[1]
  Whose wingéd glimmer of gold lured childish
    feet,
Borrowed (with bud and bird), you understand,
  To keep while moons were warm and dews were
    sweet.


Hush,—we may have them for a little yet
  Before the weird leaf-gathering frost creeps on.
Ah, loveliest time!—wherein we may regret
  The fair things going, not the sweet things gone.

[1] Fireflies.

## X.

### FOR ANOTHER'S SAKE.

Sweet, sweet? My child, some sweeter word than
   sweet,
Some lovelier word than love, I want for you.
Who says the world is bitter, while your feet
   Are left among the lilies and the dew?

. . . Ah? So some other has, this night, to fold
   Such hands as his, and drop some precious head
From off her breast as full of baby-gold?
   I, for her grief, will not be comforted.

# IN COMPANY WITH CHILDREN.

## AFTER WINGS.

This was your butterfly, you see.
  His fine wings made him vain?—
The caterpillars crawl, but he
  Passed them in rich disdain?—
My pretty boy says, "Let him be
  Only a worm again?"


Oh child, when things have learned to wear
  Wings once, they must be fain
To keep them always high and fair.
  Think of the creeping pain
Which even a butterfly must bear
  To be a worm again!

## BABY OR BIRD?

"But is he a Baby or a Bird?"
  Sometimes I fancy I do not know;
His voice is as sweet as I ever heard
  Far up where the light leaves blow.

Then his lovely eyes, I think, would see
  As clear as a Bird's in the upper air;
And his red-brown head, it seems to me,
  Would do for a Bird to bear.

"If he were a Bird," you wisely say,
  "He would have some wings to know him by:"
Ah, he has wings, that are flying away
  For ever—how fast they fly!

They are flying with him, by day, by night;
  Under suns and stars, over storm and snow,
These fair, fine wings, that elude the sight,
  In softest silence they go.

Come, kiss him as often as you may—
  Hush, never talk of this time next year,
For the same small Bird that we pet to-day,
  To-morrow is never here!

# MY BABES IN THE WOOD.

I KNOW a story, fairer, dimmer, sadder,
   Than any story painted in your books.
You are so glad? It will not make you gladder;
   Yet listen, with your pretty restless looks.

"Is it a Fairy Story?" Well, half fairy—
   At least it dates far back as fairies do,
And seems to me as beautiful and airy;
   Yet half, perhaps the fairy half, is true.

You had a baby sister and a brother,
   (Two very dainty people, rosily white,
Each sweeter than all things except the other!)
   Older yet younger—gone from human sight!

And I, who loved them, and shall love them ever,
   And think with yearning tears how each light hand
Crept toward bright bloom or berries—I shall never
   Know how I lost them. Do you understand?

Poor slightly golden heads! I think I missed them
    First, in some dreamy, piteous, doubtful way;
But when and where with lingering lips I kissed them,
    My gradual parting, I can never say.

Sometimes I fancy that they may have perished
    In shadowy quiet of wet rocks and moss,
Near paths whose very pebbles I have cherished,
    For their small sakes, since my most lovely loss.

I fancy, too, that they were softly covered
    By robins, out of apple-flowers they knew,
Whose nursing wings in far home sunshine hovered,
    Before the timid world had dropped the dew.

Their names were—what yours are! At this you wonder.
    Their pictures are—your own, as you have seen;
And my bird-buried darlings, hidden under
    Lost leaves—why, it is your dead selves I mean!

# MY GHOST.

[A STORY TOLD TO MY LITTLE COUSIN KATE.]

Yes, Katie, I think you are very sweet,
   Now that the tangles are out of your hair,
And you sing as well as the birds you meet,
   That are playing, like you, in the blossoms there.
But now you are coming to kiss me, you say:
   Well, what is it for? Shall I tie your shoe,
Or loop your sleeve in a prettier way?
   ——Do I know about ghosts? Indeed I do.

Have I seen one? Yes: last evening, you know,
   We were taking a walk that you had to miss,
(I think you were naughty and cried to go,
   But, surely, you'll stay at home after this!)
And, away in the twilight lonesomely
   ("What is the twilight?" It's—getting late!)
I was thinking of things that were sad to me—
   There, hush! you know nothing about them, Kate

Well, we had to go through the rocky lane,
   Close to that bridge where the water roars

By a still, red house, where the dark and rain
  Go in when they will at the open doors;
And the moon, that had just waked up, looked through
  The broken old windows and seemed afraid,
And the wild bats flew and the thistles grew
  Where once in the roses the children played.

Just across the road by the cherry-trees
  Some fallen white stones had been lying so long,
Half hid in the grass, and under these
  There were people dead. I could hear the song
Of a very sleepy dove, as I passed
  The graveyard near, and the cricket that cried;
And I looked (ah! the Ghost is coming at last!)
  And something was walking at my side.

It seemed to be wrapped in a great dark shawl,
  (For the night was a little cold, you know).
It would not speak. It was black and tall;
  And it walked so proudly and very slow.
Then it mocked me—everything I could do:
  Now it caught at the lightning-flies like me;
Now it stopped where the elder-blossoms grew;
  Now it tore the thorns from a grey bent tree.

Still it followed me under the yellow moon,
  Looking back to the graveyard now and then,
Where the winds were playing the night a tune——
  But, Kate, a Ghost does n't care for *men*,
And your papa *could n't* have done it harm!
  . . . Ah, dark-eyed darling, what is it you see?
There, you need n't hide in your dimpled arm—
  It was only my Shadow that walked with me!

---

## THE END OF THE RAINBOW.

MAY you go to find it? You must, I fear;
  Ah, lighted young eyes, could I show you how——
"Is it past those lilies that look so near?"
  It is past all flowers. Will you listen, now?

The pretty new moons faded out of the sky,
  The bees and butterflies out of the air,
And sweet wild songs would flutter and fly
  Into wet dark leaves and the snow's white glare.

There were winds and shells full of lonesome cries,
  There were lightnings and mists along the way,
And the deserts would glitter against my eyes,
  Where the beautiful phantom-fountains play.

At last, in a place very dusty and bare,
  Some little dead birds I had petted to sing,
Some little dead flowers I had gathered to wear,
  Some withered thorns and an empty ring,

Lay scattered. My fairy story is told.
  (It does not please her: she has not smiled.)
What is it you say?—Did I find the gold?
  Why, I found the End of the Rainbow, child!

## THE HIGHEST MOUNTAIN.

I KNOW of a higher Mountain. Well?
"Do the flowers grow on it?" No, not one.
"What is its name?" But I cannot tell.
"Where——?" Nowhere under the sun!

"Is it under the moon, then?" No, the light
  Has never touched it, and never can;
It is fashioned and formed of night, of night
  Too dark for the eyes of man.

Yet I sometimes think, if my Faith had proved
  As a grain of mustard seed to me,
I could say to this Mountain: "Be thou removed,
  And be thou cast in the sea!"

## PLAYING BEGGARS.

"Let us pretend we are two beggars." "No,
   For beggars are im—— something, something bad;
You *know* they are, because Papa says so,
   And Papa when he calls them that looks mad;
You should have seen him, how he frowned one day,
When Mama gave his wedding-coat away."

"Well, now he can't get married any more,
   Because he has no wedding-coat to wear.
But that poor ragged soldier at the door
   Was starved to death in prison once somewhere,
And shot dead somewhere else, and it was right
To give him coats—because he had to fight.

"Now let's be beggars." "They're im—postors.
    Yes,
   That's what they are, im—postors; and that means
Rich people, for they all *are* rich, I guess—
   Richer than we are, rich as Jews or queens,
And *they're* just playing beggars when they cry——"
"Then let us play like they do, you and I."

"Well, we'll be rich and wear old naughty clothes."
  "But they're *not* rich. If they were rich they'd buy
All the fine horses at the fairs and shows
  To give to General Grant. I'll *tell* you why:
Once when the rebels wanted to kill all
The men in this *world—he* let Richmond fall!


"*That* broke them up! I like the rebels, though,
  Because they have the curliest kind of hair.
One time, so many years and years ago,
  I saw one over in Kentucky there.
It showed me such a shabby sword, and said
It wanted to cut off—Somebody's head!


"But—*do* play beggar. You be one; and, mind,
  Shut up one eye, and get all over dust,
And say this:
        'Lady, be so very kind
  As to give me some water. Well, I must
Rest on your step, I think, ma'am, for a while——
I've walked full twenty if I've walked one mile.


"'Lady, this is your little girl, I know:
  She is a beautiful child—and just like you;

You look too young to be her mother, though.
　This handsome boy is like his father, too :
The gentleman was he who passed this way
And looked so cross ?—so pleasant, I should say!

"'But trouble, Lady, trouble puts me wrong.
　Lady, I'm sure you'll spare a dress or two—
You look so stylish.　(Oh, if I was strong!)
　And shoes ? Yours are too small. I need them new.
The money——thank you!　Now you have some tea,
And flour, and sugar, you'll not miss, for me ?

"'Ah, I forgot to tell you that my house
　Was burned last night.　My baby has no bread,
And I'm as poor, ma'am, as a cellar-mouse.
　My husband died once ; my grandmother's dead—
She was a good soul (but she's gone, that's true——
You have some coffee, madam ?)—so are you.'"

"Oh, it's too long.　I can't say half of *that !*
　I'll not be an im—postor, any how.
(But I should like to give one my torn hat,
　So I could get a prettier one, just now.)
They're worse than Christians, ghosts, or—anything .
——I'll play that I'm a great man or a king."

　1866.

## A CHILD'S FIRST SIGHT OF SNOW.

OH, come and look at his blue, sweet eyes,
   As, through the window, they glance around
And see the glittering white surprise
   The Night has laid on the ground!

This beautiful Mystery you have seen,
   So new to your life, and to mine so old,
Little wordless Questioner——"What does it mean?"
   Why, it means, I fear, that the world is cold.

---

## LAST WORDS.

### OVER A LITTLE BED AT NIGHT.

GOOD-NIGHT, pretty sleepers of mine—
   I never shall see you again:
Ah, never in shadow or shine;
   Ah, never in dew or in rain!

## LAST WORDS.

In your small dreaming-dresses of white,
  With the wild-bloom you gathered to-day
In your quiet shut hands, from the light
  And the dark you will wander away.

Though no graves in the bee-haunted grass,
  And no love in the beautiful sky,
Shall take you as yet, you will pass,—
  With this kiss, through these teardrops. Good-bye!

With less gold and more gloom in their hair,
  When the buds near have faded to flowers,
Three faces may wake here as fair—
  But older than yours are, by hours!

Good-night, then, lost darlings of mine—
  I never shall see you again:
Ah, never in shadow or shine;
  Ah, never in dew or in rain!

# MY ARTIST.

[A. V. P.—*Nat.* 1864.]

So slight, and just a little vain
   Of eyes and amber-tinted hair
Such as you will not see again—
   To watch him at the window there,
Why, you would not suspect, I say,
The rising rival of Doré.

No sullen lord of foreign verse
   Such as great Dante yet he knows;
No wandering Jew's long legend-curse
   On his light hand its darkness throws;
Nor has the Bible suffered much,
So far, from his irreverent touch.

Yet, can his restless pencil lack
   A master Fancy, weird and strong
In black-and-white—but chiefly black!—
   When at its call such horrors throng?

## MY ARTIST. 139

What Fantasies of Fairyland
  More shadowy were ever planned!

But giants and enchantments make
  Not all the glory of his Art:
His vast and varied power can take
  In real things a real part.
His latest pictures here I see:
Will you not look at some with me?

First, "Alexander." From his wars,
  With arms of awful length he seems
To reach some very-pointed stars,
  As if "more worlds" were in his dreams!
But, hush—the Artist tells us why:
" You read—'His hands could touch the sky.'"[1]

Here—mark how marvellous, how new!—
  Above a drowning ship, at night,
Close to the moon the sun shines, too,
  While lightnings show in streaks of white——
Still, should my eyes grow dim, ah, then
Their tears will wet those sinking men!

[1] Line from a familiar child's poem in a school-book.

There in wild weather, quite forlorn,
    And queer of cloak, and grim of hat,
With locks that might be better shorn,
    High on a steeple—who is that?
"It is the man who—I forget—
Stood on a tower in the wet."[1]


His faults? He yet is young, you know—
    Four with his last year's butterflies.
But think what wonders books may show
    When the new Tennysons arise!
For fame that he might illustrate
Let poets be content to wait!

---

[1] "I stood on a tower in the wet,
    And Old Year and New Year met."—TENNYSON.

# THE SAD STORY OF A LITTLE GIRL.

Oh, never mind her eyes and hair,
   (Though they were dark and it was gold.)
That she was sweet is all I care
   To tell you—till the rest is told.
   ——"But is the story old?"

Hush. She *was* sweet——Why do I cry?
   Because—her mother loved her so.
I told you that she did not die;
   But she is gone. "Where did she go?
   Ah me,—I do not know.

"How old was she when she was sweet?"
   Why, one year old, or two, or three.
Here is her shoe—what little feet!
   And yet they walked away, you see.
   (I must not say, from me.)

"Did Gypsies take her?" Surely, no.
   But—something took her; she is lost:
No track of hers in dew or snow,

No heaps of wild buds backward tossed,
To show what paths she crossed.

"Did Fairies take her?" It may be.
　For Fairies sometimes, I have read,
Will climb the moonshine, secretly,
　To steal a baby from its bed,
　And leave an imp instead.

This Changeling, German tales declare,
　Makes trouble in the house full soon:
Cries at the tangles in its hair,
　Beats the piano out of tune,
　And—wants to sleep till noon.

And, while it keeps the lost one's face,
　It grows less lovely, year by year——
Yes, in that pretty baby's place
　There was a Changeling left, I fear.
　. . . My little maid, do you hear?

## AT HANS ANDERSEN'S FUNERAL.

Why, all the children in all the world had listened around his knee,
    But the wonder-tales must end;
So, all the children in all the world came into the church to see
    The still face of their friend.

"But were any fairies there?" Why, yes, little questioner of mine,
    For the fairies loved him too;
And all the fairies in all the world, as far as the moon can shine,
    Sobbed, "Oh! what shall we do?"

Well, the children who played with the North's white swans, away in the North's white snows,
    Made wreaths of fir for his head;
And the South's dark children scattered the scents of the South's red rose
    Down at the feet of the dead.

Yes, all the children in all the world were there with
 their tears that day;
   But the boy who loved him best,
Alone in a damp and lonesome place (not far from
 his grave) he lay—
   And sadder than all the rest.


"Mother," he moaned, "never mind the king—why,
 what if the king is there ?
   Never mind your faded shawl:
The king may never see it; for the king will hardly
 care
   To look at your clothes at all."


So, close to his coffin she crouched, in the breath of
 the burial flowers,
   And begged for a bud or a leaf:—
"If I cannot have one, O sirs, to take to that poor
 little room of ours,
   My boy will die of his grief!"


My child, if the king *was* there, and I think he was
 (but then I forget),
   Why, that *was* a little thing.

Did a dead man ever lift his head from its place in
    the coffin yet,
        Do you think, to bow to the king?

'But could he not see him up in Heaven?" I never
    was there, you know;
        But Heaven is too far, I fear,
For the ermine, and purple, and gold, that make up
    the king, to show
        So bravely as they do here.

But he saw the tears of the peasant-child, by the
    beautiful light he took
        From the earth in his close-shut eyes;
For tears are the sweetest of all the things we shall
    see, when we come to look
        From the windows of the skies.

# A COAT-OF-ARMS.

ROSE says her family is so old—
   Older than yours, perhaps? Ah, me!
. . . (How wise she is! Who could have told
   So much to such a child as she?

If these sweet sisters teach her this,
   Their veils are vanity, I fear.) . . .
Pray, what comes next, my lovely miss?
  —— You want a coat-of-arms, my dear!

Ah!—other people have such things?
   Rose had ancestors, too—an earl?
Tell Rose you have the blood of kings,
   And show it—when you blush, my girl!

I am not jesting; I could name,
   Among the greatest, one or two
Who have the right (divine) to claim
   Remote relationship with you.

Alfred—who never burned a cake!
Arthur—who had no Table Round,
Nor knight like Launcelot of the Lake,
  Nor ruled one rood of British ground!

Lear, who outraved the storm—at most
  The crown is straw that crowns old age;
And Hamlet's father——he's a ghost?
  A real ghost, though—on the stage!

Edwards and Henrys—and of these
  Old Bluebeard Hal, from whom you take
Your own bluff manners, if you please!
  —— Let's love him, for Queen Catherine's sake!

Richard from Holy Land, who heard—
  Or did not hear—poor Blondel's song;
That other Richard, too, the Third,
  Whom Shakespeare does a grievous wrong;

But—still he murdered in the Tower
  The pretty princes? Charles, whose head,
At Cromwell's breath, fell as a flower
  Falls at the frost—as I have read.

Another Charles, who had the crown
    Of Spain and Germany to hold,
But at a cloister laid it down,
    And kept two hollow hands to fold.


Philip the Handsome, who will rise
    From his old grave, the legends say,
And show the sun those Flemish eyes
    That——yes, I mean at Judgment Day.


Louis the Grand——Madam is so
    Like some one at his court, you hear?
These Washington reporters, though,
    Were never at his court, I fear!


Great Frederick, with his snuff (I may
    Say something of great Peter, too),
And one who made kings out of clay,
    And lost the world at Waterloo!


Of others, more than I could write,—
    In some still cave scarce known to men
One sleeps, in his long beard's red light,
    A hundred years—then sleeps again;

One—who with all his peerage fell
   By Fontarabia—sat forlorn
In jewelled death at Aix——ah! well,
   Who listens now for Roland's horn?

One who was half a god, they say,
   Cried for the stars—and died of wine;
One pushed the crown of Rome away—
   And Antony's speech was very fine!

. . . The Shah of Persia, too? Why, yes,
   He and his overcoat, no doubt.
—— Oh, the Khedive will send, I guess,
   Half Egypt[1]—when he finds you out!

Victor of Italy, the Czar,
   Franz-Joseph, the sweet Spanish youth,
And Prussian William,—these are all
   Your kinsmen, child, in very truth.

Your coat-of-arms, then——I forgot
   Some kings, the oldest, wisest, best;—
Take Jason's golden fleece,—why not?
   Put Solomon's seal upon your crest.

[1] Allusion to the Khedive's present to an American lady, 1875.

There I can prove your Family's ties
    Bind you to all the great, I trust:
Its Founder lived in Paradise;
    And his ancestor was—the Dust.

Can Rose say more? . . . Your ancient Tree
    Must hold a sword of fire (its root
Down in the very grave must be)
    With serpent and—Forbidden Fruit.

---

## HIDING THE BABY.

Hold him close, and closer hold him.
    (Ah, but this is time to cry!)
Bring his pretty cloak and fold him
    From the Old Man going by.
What Old Man?—you cannot guess?
    Not the Old Man of the Sea,
Nor the Mountains, I confess,
    Can be half so old as he.

## HIDING THE BABY.

Could we only catch and bind him,
    To some prison, shutting low,
Where the sun could never find him,
    This Old Man should surely go.
We would steal his scythe away,
    (Grass should grow about our feet,)
And he should not take to-day
    From us while to-day was sweet.

Gypsy ways he has, most surely,
    (Gypsy ways are hardly right;)
Wandering, stealing, yet securely
    Keeping somehow out of sight.
From our trees the fruit he shakes;
    Silver, lace, or silk we miss
From our houses; this he takes—
    This, and other things than this.

Here he comes with buds that wither;
    Here he comes with birds that fly;
Pretty playthings he brings hither,
    Just to take them by and by.
He could find you in the night,
    Though you should put out the moon—
He can see without a light,
    He will take the Baby soon.

Head with gold enough about it
  Just to light this whole world through;
Ah, what shall we do without it?—
  Children, say, what shall we do?
Tell me, is there any place
  We can hide the Baby? Say.
Can we cover up his face
  While the Old Man goes this way?


There is one place, one place only,
  We can hide him if we must—
Very still and low and lonely;
  We can cover him with dust—
Shut a wild rose in his hand;
  Set a wild rose at his head;
This Old Man, you understand,
  Cannot take from us the dead.

# THE LITTLE BOY I DREAMED ABOUT.

[TO ANOTHER LITTLE BOY.]

THIS is the only world I know—
   It is in this same world, no doubt.
Ah me, but I could love him so,
   If I could only find him out,—
   The Little Boy I dreamed about!

This Little Boy, who never takes
   The prettiest orange he can see,
The reddest apple, all the cakes
   (When there are twice enough for three,)—
   Where can the darling ever be?

*He* does not tease and storm and pout
   To climb the roof, in rain or sun,
And pull the pigeon's feathers out
   To see how it will look with none,
   Or fight with hornets—one to one!

*He* does not hide, and cut his hair,
    And wind the watches wrong, and cry
To throw the kitten down the stair
    And see how often it can die.
    (It's strange that you can wonder why!)


*He* never wakes too late to know
    A bird is singing near his bed:
He tells the tired moon: "You may go
    To sleep yourself." *He* never said,
    When told to do a thing, "Tell Fred!"


If I say "Go," *he* will not stay
    To lose his hat, or break a toy;
Then hurry like the wind away,
    And whistle like the wind for joy,
    To please himself—this Little Boy.


Let any stranger come who can,
    *He* will not say—though it be true—
"Old Lady" (or "Old Gentleman"),
    "I wish you would go home, I do;
    I think my mama wants you to!"

—No, Fairyland is far and dim:
  He does not play in silver sand;
But if I could believe in him
  I could believe in Fairyland,
  Because——you do not understand.


Dead—dead? Somehow I do not know.
  The sweetest children die. We may
Miss some poor footprint from the snow,
  That was his very own to-day——
  "God's will" is what good Christians say.


Like you, or you, or you can be
  When you are good, he looks, no doubt.
I'd give—the goldenest star I see
  In all the dark to find him out,
  The Little Boy I dreamed about!

# CALLING THE DEAD.

My little child, so sweet a voice might wake
So sweet a sleeper for so sweet a sake;
Calling your buried brother back to you
You laugh and listen—till I listen too.

. . . Why does he listen? It may be to hear
Sounds too divine to reach my troubled ear;
Why does he laugh? It may be he can see
The face that only tears can hide from me.

Poor baby faith, so foolish or so wise:—
The name I shape out of forlornest cries
He speaks as with a bird's or blossom's breath.
How fair the knowledge is that knows not Death!

. . . Ah, fools and blind!—through all the piteous
      years
Searchers of stars and graves—how many seers,
Calling the dead, and seeking for a sign,
Have laughed and listened, like this child of mine?

## THE LAMB IN THE SKY.

"THERE is a lamb," the children said;—
   Sweet in the grass they saw it lie.
But the Baby lifted his golden head,
   And looked for the lamb in the sky.


Then the children laughed as they saw him look
   At the high white clouds, but I know not why,—
For (have I not read in a beautiful Book?)
   There *is* a Lamb in the sky.

## "I WANT IT YESTERDAY."

"Come, take the flower—it is not dead;
　'Twas kept in dew the soft night through."
"I will not have it now," he said:
　"I want it yesterday, I do."

"It is as red, it is as sweet"—
　With angry tears he turned away,
Then flung it fiercely at his feet,
　And said, "I want it—yesterday!"

---

## INTO THE WORLD AND OUT.

Into the world he looked with sweet surprise.
The children laughed so when they saw his eyes.

Into the world a rosy hand in doubt
He reached;—a pale hand took one rosebud out.

"And that was all?"—quite all, it may be. . . . But
The children cried so when his eyes were shut.

## THE BABY'S BROTHER.

The Baby is brought for the lady to see:
"Was ever a lily-bud nicer than he?"
But the door opens fiercely on cooing and kiss,
And—what merry outlaw from the greenwood is this?

His brother?—who laughs at himself in my face:
This picturesque vagabond, graceless with grace,
Whose head, like a king's come to grief, is dis-
    crowned——
Ah, the kitten was wicked, and so she is drowned?

All flushed with the butterfly chase, how he stands,
With a nestful of birds in his pitiless hands,
Which he mildly assures me were torn from the tree,
Or they'd trouble their mother as Baby does me!

"Well, if Baby *is* sweet, you must love him right fast,
Because——don't you know? Why, because he'll
    not last!
For I was a baby, too, some of these days,
And just look at me *now!*" he unsparingly says.

## CHILD'S-FAITH.

THESE beautiful tales, I trust, are true.
    But here is a grave in the moss,
And there is the sky. And the buds are blue,
    And a butterfly blows across.

Yes, here is the grave and there is the sky;—
    To the one or the other we go.
And between them wavers the butterfly,
    Like a soul that does not know,

Somewhere? Nowhere? Too-golden head,
    And lips that I miss and miss,
You would tell me the secret of the dead—
    Could I find you with a kiss!

. . . Come here, I say, little child of mine,
    Come with your bloom and breath.
(If he should believe in the life divine,
    I will not believe in death!)

"Where is your brother?"—I question low,
    And wait for his wise reply.
Does he say, "Down there in the grave?" Ah, no;—
    He says, with a laugh, "In the sky!"

# THE FUNERAL OF A DOLL.

THEY used to call her Little Nell,
In memory of that lovely child
Whose story each had learned to tell.
  She, too, was slight and still and mild,
  Blue-eyed and sweet; she always smiled,
And never troubled any one
Until her pretty life was done.
And so they tolled a tiny bell
  That made a wailing fine and faint,
As fairies ring, and all was well.
  Then she became a waxen saint.

Her funeral it was small and sad.
  Some birds sang bird-hymns in the air.
The humming-bee seemed hardly glad,
  Spite of the honey everywhere.
  The very sunshine seemed to wear
Some thought of death, caught in its gold
That made it waver wan and cold.
Then, with what broken voice he had,
  The preacher slowly murmured on
(With many warnings to the bad)
  The virtues of the darling gone.

A paper coffin rosily-lined
  Had Little Nell. There, drest in white,
With buds about her, she reclined,
  A very fair and piteous sight—
  Enough to make one sorry, quite.
And, when at last the lid was shut
Under white flowers, I fancied——but
No matter. When I heard the wind
  Scatter Spring-rain that night across
The doll's wee grave, with tears half-blind
  One child's heart felt a grievous loss.

"It was a funeral, Mama. Oh,
  Poor Little Nell is dead, is dead!
How dark!—and do you hear it blow?
  She is afraid." And as she said
  These sobbing words, she laid her head
Between her hands, and whispered: "Here
Her bed is made, the precious dear—
She cannot sleep in it, I know.
  And there is no one left to wear
Her pretty clothes. Where did she go?
  ... See, this poor ribbon tied her hair!"

## ONE YEAR OLD.

So, now he has seen the sun and the moon,
    The flower and the falling leaf on the tree
(Ah! the world is a picture that's looked at soon),
    Is there anything more to see?


He has learned (let me kiss from his eyes that tear),
    As the children tell me, to creep and to fall;—
Then life is a lesson that's taught in a year,
    For the Baby knows it all.

## ABOUT A MAGICIAN.

OH, there is a magician that I know,
   As strange as Hermann is——"But he can wring
A white bird's neck off in the market, though,
   Then—put it on and tell the bird to sing
                 And fly like anything!

"What can *he* do?" Just wait and see him pass,
   And you shall see, I think, what you shall see.
The pretty baby, creeping in the grass,
   Will be a naughty boy, and climb a tree,
                 If he goes by—ah, me!

Why, men and women in his path will rise—
   Yes, of the dust, or nothing, they are made.
We see them in the sun with real eyes,
   And, while we look at them, he makes them fade
                 To ghosts——You are afraid?

Then, he can pass the guards in any light,
   And take the palace and the king away.
He has not gone to sleep a single night,
   For many million years—some people say,—
                 Nor rested for a day!

We cannot kill him—though we sometimes try;
   He kills us all——yes, and the soldiers, too!
Seas are not deep enough to drown him. I
   Have heard that fire is—what he passes through
          Look, he is changing you!

Why, in a little while you will not be
   Yourself. And then——What will he change you
  to,
Poor, yellow-headed child, here at my knee
   Waiting to hear a foolish story through?
          Ah, Fred, what if we knew!


## FORGIVENESS.

Go, show the bee that stung your hand
The sweetest flower in all the land;

Then, from its bosom, she will bring
The honey that will cure the sting.

# EVERYTHING.

[A FAIRY TALE.]

You'd call his room a pleasant place:
Satin and rose-wood, lights and lace,
And fruits and wines were there.  (Ah, well!)
And yet the rich man rang his bell,—
When lo! he saw a fairy flit
From outside dusk to answer it.

Her flower-like eyes, so faint and blue,
Looked at him through her veil of dew;
Though every gracious thing he had,
His face was fretful, tired, and sad:—
"Pray, sir," she whispered, "did you ring?"
He said: "Yes, I want—everything!"

The fairy laughed and walked away.
Ragged and rosy at his play,
A boy who had the grass, the dew,
Birds, bees, the sun, the stars, like you,
She met: "What do you want?" sighed she.
"Oh, I have everything!" said he.

# LITTLE CHRISTIAN'S TROUBLE.

His wet cheeks looked as they had worn,
    Each, with its rose, a thorn,

Set there (my boy, you understand?)
    By his own brother's hand:

"Look at my cheek. What shall I do?—
    You know I have but two!"

His mother answered, as she read
    What my Lord Christ had said,

(While tears began to drop like rain:)
    "Go, turn the two again."

# MIDSUMMER-NIGHT FAIRIES.

(THE FIREFLIES.)

LET'S see: We believe in wings,
  We believe in the grass and dew,
We believe in the moon—and other things
  That may be true.

But are there any? Talk low;
  (Look! what is that eerie spark?)
If there *are* any, why, there they go,
  Out in the dark!

# MISCELLANEOUS.

## HEARING THE BATTLE.

### [JULY 21, 1861.]

ONE day in the dreamy summer,
   On the Sabbath hills, from afar
We heard the solemn echoes
   Of the first fierce words of war.

Ah, tell me, thou veiléd Watcher
   Of the storm and the calm to come,
How long by the sun or shadow
   Till these noises again are dumb.

And soon in a hush and glimmer
   We thought of the dark, strange fight,
Whose close in a ghastly quiet
   Lay dim in the beautiful night.

Then we talked of coldness and pallor,
   And of things with blinded eyes
That stared at the golden stillness
   Of the moon in those lighted skies;

And of souls, at morning wrestling
    In the dust with passion and moan,
So far away at evening
    In the silence of worlds unknown.

But a delicate wind beside us
    Was rustling the dusky hours,
As it gathered the dewy odours
    Of the snowy jessamine-flowers.

And I gave you a spray of the blossoms,
    And said: "I shall never know
How the hearts in the land are breaking,
    My dearest, unless you go."

WASHINGTON, D. C.

## TO-DAY.

AH, real thing of bloom and breath,
    I cannot love you while you stay.
Put on the dim, still charm of death,
    Fade to a phantom, float away,
    And let me call you Yesterday!

Let empty flower-dust at my feet
   Remind me of the buds you wear;
Let the bird's quiet show how sweet
   The far-off singing made the air;
   And let your dew through frost look fair.

In mourning you I shall rejoice.
   Go: for the bitter word may be
A music—in the vanished voice;
   And on the dead face I may see
   How bright its frown has been to me.

Then in the haunted grass I'll sit,
   Half tearful in your withered place,
And watch your lovely shadow flit
   Across To-morrow's sunny face,
   And vex her with your perfect grace.

So, real thing of bloom and breath,
   I weary of you while you stay.
Put on the dim, still charm of death,
   Fade to a phantom, float away,
   And let me call you Yesterday!

# SHAPES OF A SOUL.

WHITE with the starlight folded in its wings,
   And nestling timidly against your love,
At this soft time of hushed and glimmering things,
   You call my soul a dove, a snowy dove.

If I shall ask you in some shining hour,
   When bees and odours through the clear air pass
You'll say my soul buds as a small flushed flower,
   Far off, half-hiding, in the old home-grass.

Ah, pretty names for pretty moods; and you,
   Who love me, such sweet shapes as these can see
But, take it from its sphere of bloom and dew,
   And where will then your bird or blossom be?

Could you but see it, by life's torrid light,
   Crouch in its sands and glare with fire-red wrath,
My soul would seem a tiger, fierce and bright
   Among the trembling passions in its path.

And, could you sometimes watch it coil and slide,
   And drag its colours through the dust a while,
And hiss its poison under-foot, and hide,
   My soul would seem a snake——Ah, do not smile!

Yet fiercer forms and darker it can wear;
   No matter, though, when these are of the Past,
If as a lamb in the Good Shepherd's care
   By the still waters it lie down at last.

## STONE FOR A STATUE.

### TO A SCULPTOR.

LEAVE what is white for whiter use.
   For such a purpose as your own
Would be a dreary jest, a coarse abuse,
   A bitter wrong to snowy stone.

Let the pure marble's silence hold
   Its unshaped gods, and do not break
Those hidden images divine and old,
   To-day, for one mean man's small sake!

## "I WISH THAT I COULD GO."

THEY who look backward always look through tears.
  So, very dimly, somewhere, I do see
A door that opens into lonesome years,
  Furnished with—dust and silence! What can be
Sadder than absence of fair household sights,
Belovéd pictures, warm and pleasant lights,
  In empty rooms where——Does it call to me,
That first child-voice which taught my life to know
What music meant?—
            "I wish that I could go."


I turned and kissed her—"You had better stay."
  She heard the wood-bells ring among the herds:
"I want to see so many lambs to-day,"
  She answered in her little piteous words,
Sweetly half-said and tenderly half-guessed;
"You said there was one robin with a nest
  Up in the apple-flowers. I love the birds—

Ever so many times—and you could show
Me where they sleep. I wish that I could go."


"It is too far. And here are butterflies;
 Look—one—two—three. Go, catch them if you will."
"I've seen all these too much—they hurt my eyes!
They're naughty things—they never can be still!
I would not try to catch another one
Here, in the yard, to save its life! I'd run
 After some pretty new ones on the hill
Away off—almost to the skies! And, oh!
I'd be so sweet. I wish that I could go."


Nor was it only toward the clear white light,
 Led subtly on by many a violet,
She would have followed me. The great fierce Night
 Might lie beside our cottage, black and wet,
And make mad hungry noises. Still, if I
Thought fit to pass it, her appealing cry
 (The same that haunts me, sorrowfully, yet)
Was with me always—most forlorn and slow:
"If it *is* dark, I wish that I could go."

"If it is dark?"—what was the Dark? She knew.
　Just a brief bridge which others must have passed—
With a slight shiver, it might be—into
　A glitter of lamps: a life whose heart beat fast
Under sweet colours, jewels, music, all
The showers of fairy gifts that, faërily, fall
　On some Strange City, where——Oh! faint and vast,
Time lies behind, yet nearer seems to grow
That eager sound:
　　　　　　　"I wish that I could go."


It is in my own soul. Myself a child,
　Some ghostly doorway with my grief I fill;
Eager for blossoms beautiful and wild
　Just out of reach: eager to climb some hill,
So far away and almost to the skies,
And (tired of old ones) find new butterflies.
　Some One seems gone whom I would follow still.
Across the Dark I see your charmèd glow,
Strange City, shine——
　　　　　　　"I wish that I could go."

## COUNTING THE GRAVES.

"How many graves are in this world?" "Oh, child,"
   His mother answered, "surely there are two."
Archly he shook his pretty head and smiled:
   "I mean in this whole world, you know I do."

"Well, then, in this whole world: in East and West
   In North and South, in dew and sand and snow,
In all sad places where the dead may rest:
   There are two graves—yes, there are two, I know."

"But graves have been here for a thousand years,—
   Or, for ten thousand? Soldiers die, and kings;
And Christians die—sometimes." "My own poor
      tears
   Have never yet been troubled by these things.

. . . "More graves within the hollow ground, in
      sooth,
   Than there are stars in all the pleasant sky?—
Where did you ever learn such dreary truth,
   Oh, wiser and less selfish far than I?"

"I did not know,—I who had light and breath:
    Something to touch, to look at, if no more.
Fair earth to live in, who believes in death,
    Till, dumb and blind, he lies at one's own door?

. . . "I did not know—I may have heard or read—
    Of more; but should I search the wide grass through,
Lift every flower and every thorn," she said,
    "From every grave—oh, I should see but two!"

# A DEAD MAN'S FRIENDS.

[IN A HOUSE AT WASHINGTON.]

GATHERED from many lands,
A company still and strange,
In the shadow of velvet and oak—
Not one to another spoke;
With faces that did not change,
Weird with the night and dim,
They were looking their last on him.

If ever men were wise,
If ever women were fair,
If ever glory was dust
In a world of moth and rust,
Why, this and these were there;—
Guests of the great, ah, me,
How cold is your courtesy!

Does the loveliest lady of all
Drop Titian's light from her hair,
Down into his darkened eyes,—
His, who in his coffin lies?

Does that crouching Venus care
That he must forget the charm
Of her broken beautiful arm?

Yet these were the dead man's friends,—
Wooed in his passionate youth,
And won when his head was grey;
Look at them close, I pray.
Ah, these he has loved, in sooth,
Yet among them all, I fear,
Is nothing so sweet as—a tear!

## HIS SHARE AND MINE.

He went from me so softly and so soon.
His sweet hands rest at morning and at noon;

The only task God gave them was to hold
A few faint rosebuds—and be white and cold.

His share of flowers he took with him away;
No more will blossom here so fair as they.

His share of thorns he left—and, if they tear
My hands instead of his, I do not care.

His sweet eyes were so clear and lovely, but
To look into the world's wild light and shut:

Down in the dust they have their share of sleep;
Their share of tears is left for me to weep.

His sweet mouth had its share of kisses—Oh!
What love, what anguish, will he ever know?

Its share of thirst, and murmuring, and moan,
And cries unsatisfied, shall be my own.

He had his share of summer. Bird and dew
Were here with him—with him they vanished, too.

His share of dying leaves, and rains, and frost,
I take, with every dreary thing he lost.

The phantom of the cloud he did not see
For evermore shall overshadow me.

He, in return, with small, still, snowy feet,
Touched the Dim Path, and made its twilight sweet.

## THE BIRD IN THE BRAIN.

IN a legend of the East there sits
   A bird with never a mate :
Out of the dead man's brain it flits,—
   Too late for a prayer, too late,
      Repeating all the sin
      Which the beating heart shut in.

Little child of mine, that I kiss and fold,
   With your flower-like hand at my breast,
Already within this head all gold
   That bird is building a nest !
      May it give but one brief cry,
      Sweet, when you come to die.

My lord, the king, that shadowy bird
   Broods under your crown, I fear ;
Take care, sir priest, lest you whisper a word
   That Heaven were loth to hear :—
      Ermine nor lawn will it spare ;
      Ah, king, ah, priest, take care !

Oh, half-saint sister, so cloister-pale,
  That bird will be at your bier.
Though you count your beads, though you wear your veil,
  Though you hold your cross right dear,
      When your funeral tapers come
      Will the weird of wing be dumb?

Poor lover, beware of the bud of the rose
  In the maiden's hand at your side:
She has some secret, the dark bird knows,
  Which her youth's fair hair can hide,
      Turn, maid, from your lover, too—
      The bird knows more than you!

## A PRETTIER BOOK.

"He has a prettier book than this,"
    With many a sob between, he said;
Then left untouched the night's last kiss,
    And, sweet with sorrow, went to bed.

A prettier book his brother had?—
    Yet wonder-pictures were in each.
The different colours made him sad:
    The equal value—could I teach?

Ah, who is wiser? . . . Here we sit,
    Around the world's great hearth, and look,
While Life's fire-shadows flash and flit,
    Each wistful in another's book.

I see, through fierce and feverish tears,
    Only a darkened hut in mine;
Yet in my brother's book appears
    A palace where the torches shine.

A peasant, seeking bitter bread
   From the unwilling earth to wring,
Is in my book; the wine is red,
   There in my brother's, for the king.

A wedding, where each wedding-guest
   Has wedding garments on, in his,—
In mine one face in awful rest,
   One coffin never shut, there is!

In his, on many a bridge of beams
   Between the faint moon and the grass,
Dressed daintily in dews and dreams,
   The fleet midsummer fairies pass;

In mine unearthly mountains rise,
   Unearthly waters foam and roll,
And—stared at by its deathless eyes—
   The master sells the fiend a soul!

. . . Put out the lights. We will not look
   At pictures any more. We weep,
"My brother has a prettier book,"
   And, after tears, we go to sleep.

## ASKING FOR TEARS.

OH, let me come to Thee in this wild way,
Fierce with a grief that will not sleep, to pray
Of all Thy treasures, Father, only one,
After which I may say—Thy will be done.

Nay, fear not Thou to make my time too sweet.
I nurse a Sorrow,—kiss its hands and feet,
Call it all piteous, precious names, and try,
Awake at night, to hush its helpless cry.

The sand is at my moaning lip, the glare
Of the uplifted desert fills the air;
My eyes are blind and burning, and the years
Stretch on before me. Therefore, give me Tears!

## "A LETTER FROM TO-MORROW."

[THE WORDS OF A CHILD.]

THE child stood sweet and shy:
"Now listen,—do not cry:
'A Letter from To-morrow——'" he piteously said;
Then wavered, frowned, and blushed,
And looked away and hushed
The elfin voice that spoke through lips of human red.

"I cannot read the rest,"
He prettily confessed,
"Because—it is not plain!" Ah, would I hear it read?
Poor little hands, to hold
A thing so dim and cold,
So full of sad shorn hair and last words of the dead!

Let it go where it will,
There must be news of ill
Send it to that great house across the shining street:—

To-night, in lights and lace,
There Madam holds her place,
Brief as the foreign flowers that drop dead at her feet.

Madonna-hair and eyes
Remind one of the skies,
(No other picture there more subtly hides its paint).
Divinely of the earth !—
That last dear dress from Worth
Is too Parisian, perhaps, to fit a saint.

This Letter's shadowy date,
"To-morrow," folds her fate—
(Reach for it, eager arm, so beautiful and bare !)
She reads : "Your hair is grey,
And men forget the day—
Can you remember it ?—the day when you were fair !'

He reads—her stately lord,
Out-glittering some chance sword,
Or right new gold, perhaps, wherewith his name was made :
"Taken as in a snare !—
Called by a bird of the air
To justice, go and give and take it, O betrayed !"

Still keep the Letter there:—
His boy, the gracious heir
To beauty, love, and hope—a brave enough estate,—
Lets fall his toys and reads,
"Wounded to death!" and heeds.
A coffin for white flowers stands ready at the gate.

Give her the Letter—see
How fairy-sweet is she,
His girl in her first youth! She droops her flower-like head,
To read—no charmèd tale
Of bridal buds and veil;
But finds a broken ring and leave to earn her bread.

Take, now, the Letter where
There's music in the air,
And let the poet read: "The worm likes well your book."
Painter, if you are he,
Master that is to be,
Your name is not in all this Letter,—only look!

Some scented page will bring
This Letter to the king;
To-morrow will be smooth with him and loyal-sweet:

"Your throne is shaken, sire—
Your palace lost in fire;
Your prince must hide with sand the far tracks of his
feet!"

Shut close your Letter, child.
The wind is weird and wild—
I give it to the wind to bury in the sea,
Full fathom five, and pray
That till the Judgment Day
No fisherman may bring such treasure up to me!

## THE DEAD BOOK.

AH, from the yellow pages Time has torn
　The wonder-pictures seen by clearer eyes,
And from the withered words the soul is worn!
　. . . Kiss the Dead Book, and leave it where it lies.

Kiss the Dead Book, and leave it in its place——
　Youth's breathless bloom and dusty dreams among.
I read, where shining poems show no grace,
　This dreary line, "You are no longer young."

# SONGS.

## REPROOF TO A ROSE.

Sad rose, foolish rose,
  Fading on the floor,
Will he love you while he knows
  There are many more
  At the very door?


Sad rose, foolish rose,
  One among the rest:
Each is lovely—each that blows;
  It must be confest
  None is loveliest.


Sad rose, foolish rose,
  Had you known to wait,
And with dead leaves or with snow
  Come alone and late—
  Sweet had been your fate!

Sad rose, foolish rose,
　If no other grew
In the wide world, I suppose
　My own lover, too,
Would love—only you!


## WHEN THE FULL MOON'S LIGHT IS BURNING.

WHEN the full moon's light is burning
　At its brightest, it is pleasant,
Sometimes, blindly to sit yearning
　For the slightness of the crescent;

When the finished rose is shining
　In the sun with flushed completeness,
For the vanished bud repining,
　Wilfully to miss its sweetness.

# THE SONG NO BIRD SHOULD SING IN VAIN.

THE song no bird should sing in vain,
The song no bird will sing again,
I did not hear until the fleet
Air-singer lost it at my feet.

The wind that blew the enchanted scent
From some divine still continent,
Beat long against my window, but
It found and left my window shut.

The king's fair son, who came in state,
With my lost slipper, for its mate,
I only saw through my regret—
Oh, I am in the ashes yet!

# COME, WAILING WINDS; COME, BIRDS OF NIGHT.

Come, wailing winds; come, birds of night;
   Come, Time, and bring the ivy vine
To wind in constant clasp and bright
   This desolated pride of mine;—
Come with your mildew and your mould
   For these rich draperies, these fair halls;
Come with your mosses, and enfold
   These humbled towers, these broken walls!

## SAD SPRING-SONG.

BLUSH and blow, blush and blow,
  Wind and wild-rose, if you will;
You are sweet enough, I know—
You are sweet enough, but, oh!
Lying lonely, lying low,
  There is something sweeter still.

Come and go, come and go,
  Suns of morning, moons of night;
You are fair enough, I know—
You are fair enough, but oh!
Hidden darkly, hidden low,
  . Lies the light that gave you light.

## SAY THE SWEET WORDS.

SAY the sweet words, say them soon;
   You have said the bitter,—
Changed to tears, by this still moon
   You may see them glitter.

Say the sweet words soon, I pray—
   Mine is piteous pleading:
Haste to draw the steel away,
   Though the wound keep bleeding.

## FULFILMENT.

He who can sing a song more sweet
  Than skylarks learn in finest air,
Hears subtler music at his feet
  Hum in the grass—at his despair.

He who has found a sudden star,
  With new, quick halos for his head,
Sighs for some brighter one afar,
  That sits for ever veiled, instead.

He who has dared, though half-afraid,
  To make such beauty of the stone
As God from dust has never made,
  At last looks on it with a moan.

And she who wears such threads of lace
  As fairies might from moonshine spin,
Will find, if any flower she trace,
  The loveliest leaf was not put in.

Yet holds this world one perfect thing,
  That leaves no room to weep or pine ;
You gave it to me with a ring,
  To be for ever only mine.

---

## GOOD-BYE.

[A WOMAN'S SONG.]

GOOD-BYE, if it please you, sir, good-bye.
This is a world where the wild-swans fly.
This is a world where the thorn hangs on
When the rose, its twin, is gone, is gone.
  Good-bye—good-bye—good-bye.

Good-bye, if it please you, sir, good-bye.
You are here and away—I care not why.
This is a world where a man has his will,
A world where a woman had best be still.
  Good-bye—good-bye—good-bye.

## LIFE AND DEATH.

If I had chosen, my tears had all been dews;
  I would have drawn a bird's or blossom's breath,
Nor outmoaned yonder dove. I did not choose—
  And here is Life for me, and there is Death.

Ay, here is Life. Bloom for me, violet;
  Whisper me, Love, all things that are not true;
Sing, nightingale and lark, till I forget—
  For here is Life, and I have need of you.

So, there is Death. Fade, violet, from the land;
  Cease from your singing, nightingale and lark;
Forsake me, Love, for I without your hand
  Can find my way more surely to the dark.

# MAKING PEACE.

AFTER this feud of yours and mine
  The sun will shine;
After we both forget, forget,
  The sun will set.

I pray you think how warm and sweet
  The heart can beat;
I pray you think how soon the rose
  From grave-dust grows.

www.ingramcontent.com/pod-product-compliance
Lightning Source LLC
Chambersburg PA
CBHW020857230426
43666CB00008B/1213